AND THE WINNER IS...

Using awards programs to promote your
company and encourage your employees

JOHN LEVERENCE

Merritt Publishing
Santa Monica, California

And the Winner Is ...
Using Awards Programs to Promote Your Company and
Encourage Your Employees
First Edition, 1997
Copyright © 1997 by John Leverence

Merritt Publishing
401 Wilshire Boulevard, Suite 800
Santa Monica, CA 90401
(800) 638-7597
(310) 450-7234

Library of Congress Catalog Number: 96-075912

Leverence, John
And the Winner Is ...
Using Awards Programs to Promote Your Company and Encourage
Your Employees
Includes index.
Pages: 328

ISBN 1-56343-147-5
Printed in the United States of America.

FOR JULIE

The irony of the Information Age is that it has given new respectability to uninformed opinion.

John Lawton cited by Michael Crichton, *Airframe*

Acknowledgments

This book began 15 years ago, as shop talk with my wife about her work as the awards director for the Grammys® and mine at the Emmys®. Between the two of us, we administered 50 percent of the most important entertainment competitions in the United States— the other half being the Tonys® and the Oscars®—but we didn't have any "how to" references, other than the Grammy and Emmy rules and procedures, the training we got from our association colleagues at the Recording and Television Academies, and the hard knock school of day-to-day trial and error.

"Someone really ought to write a book about this stuff," Margaret said. "So why don't you?"

I hemmed and hawed for a decade, and finally started jotting down notes. When I met Merritt Publishing's CEO, Jan King, while we were both doing volunteer work for a charity fund-raiser—the Sports Legends Awards show that is detailed in this book—I pitched her my idea for a book about awards administration. She and Merritt editor Jim Walsh suggested that I expand it beyond a "guided tour behind the scenes at the Emmys" to a "brass-tacks how-to" for the "poor devils" at companies and associations who are "compelled by vague threats" to "handle" the awards.

As Cynthia Chaillie, Merritt's marketing director told me, "When you signed up to administer the Emmy contest, you made a career choice. For better or for worse, whatever you got, you asked for it. But most of the tens of thousands of people who run their companies' awards programs got the job dumped in their laps because nobody else understood, cared about or wanted it." Said Merritt editor Sue Elliott-Sink, "If you're going to write a book about awards administration, write it for them."

Although the dedication page of this book says it is for my daughter, Julie, the only reason she is going to read it is because I'm her dad, and she knows there will be a quiz. The book is really meant to be productive reading and reference for those "poor devils" whose human resources, public relations, business, communications or similar education and training never taught them how to break a tie in a ratings-score judging system, the relative appropriateness of narrow- and broad-based electorates, the eight most common eligibility restrictions and all the other awards "stuff" they need to know in order to increase the value of their awards programs.

Finally, I am most appreciative for the help and encouragement of my mentors and colleagues, among them my first executive director at the Television Academy, Tricia McLeod Robin; my current E.D., Dr. James L. Loper; Emmy Awards administrators Julie Shore, Barbara Chase and Louise Danton; and the indispensable awards counselors, Hank Rieger, Dixon Dern and George Sunga.

Table of Contents

Part 1 Why Awards Are Good Business

CHAPTER 1

The Power of Awards 5
- How Awards Can Make a Difference
- What Awards Can Do for Your Business
- Awards of All Kinds
- Recognizing Excellence
- Breaking Through the Clutter

CHAPTER 2

Using Awards Within Your Business 15
- The Need for Recognition
- How Many Awards Should You Give Out?
- Staying Power
- What Kind of Awards Should You Give?
- Should Money Be Part–or All–of the Award?
- Enhancing Your Business's Image
- Getting the Most Out of an Awards Program

CHAPTER 3

Giving Awards to Other Companies 33
- Magazine Awards
- Marketing Exposure
- Using Awards to Boost Sales
- Survey Says ...
- Promoting Values

CHAPTER 4

Association Awards 47

- Furthering the Group's Mission
- The Birth of the Emmy
- Important Association, Important Awards
- Depreciating an Award
- Peer Recognition
- For Members Only
- Vendor Recognition
- Local Awards
- Cash Prizes

CHAPTER 5

Charity Awards 65

- The Sports Legends Gala
- The Victor Sports Awards
- Cause Awards
- Rewarding Businesses
- The Generic "Man of the Year Award"
- Do the Right Thing

CHAPTER 6

Entering Awards Competitions 75

- Winning Awards Boosts Morale
- Throwing Your Hat Into the Ring
- Take It From the Top
- The Benefits of Competition
- Total Quality
- State-Based Awards
- ISO Certification
- Community Awards Programs
- University Awards Programs
- Business-to-Business Awards
- Magazine Awards

- Other Sources of Awards
- Reach Out and Win

Part 2 Creating Your Own Awards Program

CHAPTER 7

Planning Your Awards Program 113
- The Four Basic Elements
- Include It in the Bylaws
- The Common Elements
- Start With the Basics

CHAPTER 8

Pitfalls, Problems & Things to Avoid 119
- R-E-S-P-E-C-T
- Misperceptions & Myths
- What Is the Award For?
- Beware of Cheap Imitations
- Keeping an Awards Program in Perspective
- Be Careful Who You Reward

CHAPTER 9

Making Up the Rules 133
- Who Will Qualify?
- The Exception to the Rule
- Special Case Restrictions
- Quantity Restrictions
- Multiple Application Restrictions
- Future Eligibility Restrictions
- Principal Identity Restrictions
- Prior Achievement
- Time Frame Restrictions
- Age Restrictions
- Moral Suitability

- When Lawyers Get Involved
- Deadline? What Deadline?
- Protect Your Company
- Is There a Judge and Jury in Your Future?

CHAPTER 10

I'll Be the Judge of That 161
- What Makes a Competition?
- A Competitive Awards Process
- Non-Competitive Awards
- Hybrid Awards
- Here Comes da Judge
- Narrow- and Broad-Based Electorates
- A Two-Tier Voting Process
- Single- and Double-Pass Systems
- Judging Formats
- Non-Competitive Judging Formats
- Juried Awards
- Key Points to Consider

CHAPTER 11

Procedures for Entries and Nominees 187
- The Entry Form
- Gathering Information From Entrants
- Asking Entrants to Rate Themselves
- Grant Applications
- Crafting a Sample Entry Form
- Making Entry Forms Available
- Receipt Confirmation
- Who's Doing the Entering?
- Processing Completed Forms
- The Steps the Emmys Follow
- Program Title Proof
- Multiple Entry Proof for Programs

- Multiple Entry Proof for Individuals
- Inconsistent Categorization Proof
- Network Proof
- Production Company Proof
- Proofing for "Special Rules" Errors
- Ballot Preparation
- Ballot Distribution and Return Audits
- Dealing With Ties
- Ties in a Rating System
- Ties in a Preferential Voting Format
- And the Nominees Are ...
- Notifying the Nominees
- The Winners
- Post Mortem

CHAPTER 12

Time and Money 229

- Using Rules and Procedures to Set the Awards Calendar
- The Major Steps in the Awards Process
- Calculating the Time Required for Each Step
- Wiggle Room
- Setting the Start Date
- Using Rules and Procedures to Set the Awards Budget
- Income
- Entry Fees
- Expenditures
- Should You Pay the Judges?
- Getting to the Bottom Line

CHAPTER 13

The Awards Presentation 253

- Planning the Awards Presentation
- Elements of the Awards Presentation
- Business Awards Presentations

- Planning the Awards Presentation
- Elements of the Awards Presentation
- Business Awards Presentations
- Awards Presentation Pre-Production
- Showing Respect
- Special Event Awards Presentations
- "I'd Like to Thank the Academy ..."
- Awards Presentation Production
- Get It on Tape
- Post-Ceremony Personalization of the Awards
- Awards Presentation Do's and Don'ts

CHAPTER 14

How to Use Awards to Generate Publicity 277
- Start Sending Out Press Releases
- Announcing the Nominees
- Live Annoucement
- Inviting the Press to the Presentation
- Who to Invite
- Other Ways You Can Promote the Awards Program
- Ways Recipients Will Promote the Award
- Providing and Designing Logos
- Post-Awards Certificates
- Craft Citations
- Commemorative Awards
- The Power of Publicity

Conclusion 293
Appendix 1 297
Appendix 2 299
Appendix 3 303
Appendix 4 307
Appendix 5 313
Appendix 6 319
Index 323

PART 1

WHY
AWARDS
ARE GOOD
BUSINESS

The Power of Awards

Languishing in 87th place among 96 primetime series in the spring of 1981, *Hill Street Blues'* future on the NBC network was shaky.

But on August 6, the Academy of Television Arts & Sciences made the startling announcement that *Hill Street Blues* had garnered a record number of drama series nominations (21) for the Primetime Emmy Awards.

Five weeks later, on the CBS broadcast of the awards presentation, 66 million viewers witnessed Emmys being given to the show for writing, directing, lead actor and actress, supporting actor and the big one—outstanding drama series. Including the two technical awards won at a non-televised awards presentation, *Hill Street Blues* garnered more Emmys in its premiere season than any other series in the 33-year history of the Emmys—a record that has not been broken in the ensuing 15 years.

On that September evening in 1981, the Primetime Emmy Awards fulfilled the purpose of all awards:

to recognize accomplishment in a personal, professional or social endeavor and, by means of that recognition, afford the accomplishment an extraordinary place within its ordinary milieu.

By the end of the telecast on September 13, 1981, the Emmy Awards had positioned *Hill Street Blues* as a primetime contender. Thomas O'Neil, author of *The Emmys*, wrote, "It was the greatest and most dramatic victory in the history of the Emmys."

How Awards Can Make a Difference

How had a passel of wins on a TV awards show facilitated the revival of a faltering series?

In acceptance speech after acceptance speech, Daniel J. Travanti, Steven Bochco, Michael Conrad, Barbara Babcock and others told the audience of their passionate commitment to the show, and how honored they were to be part of it. *Hill Street Blues* was repeatedly and consistently characterized by the winners as a show to be proud of and to believe in.

This was an opinion shared by both the press and NBC, which had renewed the series for another season despite its low ratings. *Hill Street Blues'* position in the ratings doldrums of mass-market network television was a classic case of Primetime quality being out of synch with Nielsen quantity.

However, as the winners came to the stage and proudly accepted their Emmys as tangible symbols of excellence, there occurred an indisputable, nationally televised confirmation that here was an extraordinary, not-to-be-missed show.

Within a year, *Hill Street Blues* had picked up another 21 nominations. "But this time the program was not facing the same uphill battle it did before," wrote O'Neil. "One of the first great cop shows that was actually more about cops than crime had climbed significantly in the ratings over the past twelve months and was now, said the *Herald Examiner*, 'flying high.' "

By the time its last episode aired on May 19, 1987, it had set Emmy records that still stand today for drama series nominations (98) and wins (26). Moreover, it had enjoyed steady popularity with what the networks and advertisers considered television's most desirable niche audience.

A group of Emmys clearly did wonders for an ailing TV show. But what if you aren't in the entertainment industry? How can awards help your business?

What Awards Can Do for Your Business

Actually, they can help in three ways:

1) By entering an awards competition, you can publicize your business, get recognition for your company's achievements and benchmark your company in comparison with others in your industry or the world at large.

2) By creating your own awards competition, you can recognize your suppliers or other businesses—as a way of improving your company's working relationships and possibly even publicizing your company. (Just think how many times *Motor Trend* magazine's name is mentioned by car companies in their expensive, nationwide advertising campaigns, thanks to the magazine's Car of the Year Awards.)

3) By creating an internal awards program, you can recognize, reward and motivate your company's employees.

Awards can be—and have been—used by almost any type of business or organization. For instance, associations can use awards to honor individual professional achievement. And charitable organizations can use awards for the purpose of fundraising (especially if they charge big ticket prices for the awards presentation ceremony).

This book is a practical guide for the use and creation of all of these types of award programs and more. We'll discuss:

- how to use awards to motivate your work force;

- how to enter other people's awards competitions;

- how to create a set of rules that will make your awards program a success; and

- how to get the most benefit from the awards you give and the awards you win.

Awards of All Kinds

Among the various types of awards that are given, some are famous and ongoing. They include the Emmy, Oscar, Tony and Grammy; the Golden Globe, Pulitzer, Peabody and Nobel; the Malcolm Baldrige National Quality Award, Obie, Edgar, Humanitas and National Book Award; Harvard's Hasty Pudding Man and Woman of the Year Awards.

Others are defunct, but historically famous nonetheless: the Bush administration's Daily Point of Light Awards—for every American who made a positive difference—which had as its long-term goal the designation of a thousand points of light; and former Senator William Proxmire's Golden Fleece Award, "to recognize the most ridiculous, wasteful, extravagant, unnecessary expenditure of the federal taxpayers' money in the preceding month."

Then there are the many not-so-famous awards:

- The "International Mona Lisa Smiling Contest," sponsored by the Cranbrook Academy of Art in Bloomfield Hills, Michigan—win with a photograph of a person whose smile best resembles the smile of Mona Lisa in the famous painting.

- The Bald Is Beautiful Award, meant to "eliminate vanity associated with baldness and to instill pride and dignity in being baldheaded," according to the Bald Headed Men of America Association. "Criteria considered are a bald head, chrome-dome or a haircut with a hole in it." Award categories include Mr. Clean, Yul Brynner, Most Kissable and Solar Dome.

- The awards given by the Olfactory Research Fund, a nonprofit organization devoted to "establishing the positive influence of fragrance on human behavior," according to *The New Yorker*. In 1996, it awarded Coty for bringing "to the public's attention the important role of vanilla in enhancing the quality of life."

- The Hooker of the Year Award from the National Tractor Pullers Association—for the driver who has hooked (i.e., dragged a skid in competition) the most times with a single vehicle.

- The annual New Orleans prize for the contestant who best evokes Stanley Kowalski's barbaric yawp for "Stella!" With a nod to Marlon Brando, participants may wear torn T-shirts.

- The *Washington Post*'s Style Invitational, in which readers were asked to create Martha Stewart's December/January calendar. Among the top candidates' submissions was this listing for January 25: "Receive delivery of new phone books. Old ones make ideal personal address books. Simply cross out the names and addresses of all the people you do not know."

Obscure awards also can be found in spin-offs of famous awards. The Booker literary prize is England's equivalent of the premier American book award, the National Book Award, and enjoys well-deserved international renown. But, in 1994, "an organization in Britain came up with the idea of running a 'Classic Booker' contest, to run in conjunction with the current annual event," according to the Booker Prize home page on the World Wide Web. "This prize would be open to those novels published exactly 100 years ago."

The 1895 publications that reached final candidacy included *The Time Machine* by H.G. Wells and *The Red Badge of Courage* by Stephen Crane. The winner was Thomas Hardy's *Jude the Obscure*. (A film version of that book was in development at the time.)

What are the benefits of these famous or obscure awards? While the answers are as varied as the awards, it comes down to a question of fame vs. honor.

Fame has its merits. But it is respect that is the most important attribute of an award. However disparate the awards might be, the common characteristic of coveted awards is that they are a trusted recognition of excellence—excellence in making a TV series like *Hill Street Blues*, making widgets, or building and driving a winning tractor puller.

The prestige and importance that come with respect are the primary benefits for an award recipient. The Emmy Awards and *Hill Street Blues* were one case in point. Another was the awarding of the eminently prestigious National Book Award for young people's literature to first-time novelist Victor Martinez.

Before he received the award, Martinez held a reading in a San Francisco auditorium before an audience of six people. (Three were friends and three worked there.) After accepting the award before a packed house at the Grand Ballroom of the Waldorf Astoria, he found himself suddenly being pursued by literary agents and publishing opportunities. In a November 1996 *Los Angeles Times* profile titled "Plucked From the Pages of Obscurity," Martinez's situation was summed up as "... suddenly everybody's calling."

Both the Los Angeles and New York film critics announce their picks for the best movies and performances at the end of every calendar year. In effect, these announcements are the beginning of the march to the Oscars in late March. In what way are they important?

They're important because recognition breeds recognition.

"For films like *Shine* or *Crying Game*—smaller films in limited release without $20 million advertising budgets to back them up—these awards are a way of penetrating the public consciousness," Gerry Rich, president of worldwide marketing for MGM/UA, told the *Los Angeles Times* in December '96. "Last year, they created curiosity about *Leaving Las Vegas* and generated considerable editorial space. Particularly for the more discriminating art-house crowd that doesn't go to movies each week, these nods anoint a picture as a 'must-see' and uncover hidden gems. It's hard to break through the clutter, and that's where critics come in."

As things worked out, *Shine* was nominated for a 1997 Golden Globe award, and that brought it to the attention of Oscar voters. (*The English Patient* went on to win the Golden Globe.) This is historically important, because the Motion Picture Academy voters have followed the lead of the Golden Globes by at least a two-thirds margin of similarity. In the 1980s, 9 out of 10 Golden Globe best picture winners also were Oscar best picture winners. The only anomaly occurred in 1982, when *Gandhi* won the Golden Globe and *E.T.* called home with the Oscar.

The Directors Guild of America awards have a similar track record as Oscar predictors. In all but four cases since the awards began in 1949, the DGA winner has been selected best director at the Oscar telecast. The exceptions were Anthony Harvey (*The Lion in Winter*), who lost out at the Oscars to Carol Reed (*Oliver!*); Francis Ford Coppola (*The Godfather*), who lost to Bob Fosse (*Cabaret*); Steven Spielberg (*The Color*

Purple), who lost to Sydney Pollack (*Out of Africa*); and Ron Howard (*Apollo 13*), who in 1996 failed to get an Oscar nomination (the award went to Mel Gibson for *Braveheart*).

As the *Hollywood Reporter* noted in January 1997:

> Award candidates ... parlay nominations into increased boxoffice and awareness among Academy Award voters. Fine Line Features, which has domestic distribution rights to the multi-nominated Australian film *Shine*, plans additional press conferences and screenings so more press can meet the stars and see the film, as well as additional videocassette mailings to Academy of Motion Picture Arts & Sciences members, who vote on the Academy Awards.

> Said a New Line spokesman, "I feel that we've passed the first hurdle toward the Holy Grail ... the attention a Golden Globes nomination brings is a boost for the picture that money just can't buy. It raises awareness of the film and positions people into thinking about it during Academy Award nominations. It's the same thing as a quote ad. If someone else likes it, you probably will, too."

In an era when there are more movies than there are leisure hours in which to view them (or dollars to spend on the price of admission), these awards do exactly what awards are intended to do:

> Awards are meant to distinguish the extraordinary from the ordinary. They break through the clutter of our crowded popular culture. They bring recognition to the award recipient. They provide

an imprimatur of quality that guides public taste and consumption.

In short, wherever there is a field of endeavor in which standards of excellence measure degrees of accomplishment, there are—or there should be—awards.

2   Using Awards Within Your Business

If you're considering creating an awards program to enhance your business, the logical place to start is within your own company. Creating an in-house awards program is good business—in that it can be used to motivate and retain good employees. It also can serve as good practice for creating a larger and more elaborate awards program that is directed at outside individuals or other firms.

Awards typically are given by companies to employees for service, sales, safety and special achievement. These awards are separate and distinct from salary, bonuses and perks. While they may come in the form of cash prizes, they actually are meant to serve as recognition, rather than compensation.

From a company's point of view, recognizing service milestones and special achievements is more than a kind and thoughtful act. It's good business in eight specific ways. Recognition awards:

1) improve quality;

2) encourage teamwork;

3) motivate employees;

4) build morale;

5) create awareness;

6) increase loyalty;

7) decrease turnover; and

8) enhance the company's image in the community and among customers.

The Need for Recognition

According to a study published in the *Harvard Business Review*, recognition is second only to achievement as a motivation factor affecting job attitudes. What's more, the study found that recognition is over three times more important than salary as a satisfying element of work.

The Robert Half International staffing firm reached the same conclusion after polling top executives nationwide. When asked why employees typically leave a company, these executives said compensation rewards were a relatively unimportant factor. Rather, the most common reason was limited recognition and praise. Dissatisfaction with salary, raises, bonuses, limits on authority, personality conflicts with subordinates and superiors, working conditions, security and other "job quality" factors were of less importance.

Where does this need for recognition originate? It's hard-wired into us, according to psychologist A.H. Maslow. He introduced the concept of a "Hierarchy of Needs" in *Learning and Human Abilities*. At the top of this pyramid are the "esteem needs," which he described as follows:

Esteem needs most clearly suggest receiving recognition as a worthwhile person. Satisfaction of

Chapter 2—Using Awards Within Your Business

esteem needs is accompanied by feelings of confidence, worth, strength and usefulness. The thwarting of these needs produces feelings of inferiority, weakness or helplessness.

Clearly, you want your employees to feel useful, strong and confident. Workers who feel inferior, weak and helpless definitely are not going to be productive, creative and efficient.

A prime way to give outstanding employees the recognition they deserve—and crave—is by creating one or more in-house awards programs.

How Many Awards Should You Give Out?

Recognition awards come in all shapes and sizes—ranging from a brass plate on the "Employee of the Month" plaque to a service longevity pin or a banquet celebrating a completed project.

The Bruce Fox corporate recognition company designs and manufactures hundreds of thousands of what it calls "freestanding recognition accolades." Its line of Entrepreneur of the Year awards includes trophies for national and regional winners, plaques for finalists and judges, business card holders and book ends for judges' assistants, and gold-colored paperweights in the shape of the program's logo for all the nominees.

What they all have in common is that they are more than just a pat on the back for a job well done.

While some business people worry that giving out too many awards within the company dilutes their value, management experts Thomas Peters and Robert Waterman Jr. seem to have discovered just the opposite. In their study of corporate administrative effectiveness, *In Search of Excellence*, they noted that they were:

> struck by the wealth of nonmonetary incentives used by the excellent companies. Nothing is more important than positive reinforcement. Everybody uses it. But top performers, almost alone, use it extensively. The volume of opportunities for showering pins, buttons, badges and medals is staggering ... they actively pursue endless excuses to give out awards.

This is not to say that you should give an award to every employee every month. Awards still need to reward a particular occasion or type of behavior—they need to distinguish the extraordinary from the ordinary.

You also may wish to limit the number of recognition awards you give out at a particular time—particularly if those awards are going to be pricey. In limiting the number of awards to be given out at one time, you are setting up what is known as a "closed-ended" awards program.

This type of award structure often is used as an incentive for performance, such as when a company awards the salespeople who bring in the most business during a given period. It can create competition among employees, which may be productive or counterproductive—something you'll need to think long and hard about when you are drafting the rules for your awards program.

You can use a closed-ended awards program to set up a competitive situation or to reward less tangible goals. For example, Silicon Graphics, a computer manufacturer based in Mountain View, California, gives out 50 "spirit" awards each year to those employees who most embody the ideals expressed in a company poem. These ideals include "encouraging creativity" and "seeking solutions rather than blame." The 50 winners each year get a trip for two to Hawaii. Plus, they get to sit on a management advisory group for a year, giving each of the winners more control over his or her workplace destiny.

The opposite of closed-ended awards programs are "open-ended" programs, which do not place upper or lower limits on the number of awards given out. You may give out 100. Or you may not give out any. This type of award clearly is more discretionary.

You can use an open-ended awards program to reward truly extraordinary behavior. Here's a hypothetical example:

Every year, the Widget Co. pays for an employees' Christmas party. However, when one of the employees is stricken with Disease Y, Betty in accounts receivable proposes that the party fund be diverted to Charity X, which funds research to find the cure for Disease Y.

When Charity X announces that the Widget Co. will receive the Angel Award for its support of Disease Y research, President Widget decides Betty deserves an award of her own. He invites her to the board of directors meeting and presents her with a golden egg mounted atop a granite block—with "To Betty, A Good Egg" engraved on it.

President Widget thanks Betty for her compassion and thoughtfulness—"subjective" traits that are not tied to the bottom line but, in their own way, are indispensable to the company.

The Good Egg Award, in this case, was given for a special achievement. In any given period of time, the president and board of the Widget Co. may choose to award one Good Egg, more than one or none.

Staying Power

Service longevity awards are the most common type of recognition awards.

In Terryberry Co.'s "Going Beyond the Pat on the Back: A Guide to Planning Recognition and Incentive Programs," the authors point out:

> Most experts agree that tenure recognition should be given early in an employee's career, since most turnover occurs within the first five years of service. The most common programs celebrate the first, third, fifth and 10th anniversaries, then every additional fifth year. Companies in high-turnover industries, particularly retail and service firms, often present awards annually for the first five years, then adopt a schedule with longer periods between awards.

Says Betty Hogan, human resources director of Banner Pharmacaps in Chatsworth, California: "We give cash for the fifth and 10th anniversaries, then a ring for the 15th. On the day the ring is given, most employees say they would prefer cash. But a month later, when the money has been spent on who-remembers-what, they are pleased to have that ring and wear it with pride.

"One employee who left the company for another position later told me that he continued to wear his anniversary ring. He said, 'I earned it, I deserved it, and even though it is something of an anachronism in my new position, it still means a lot to me as a reminder of what I accomplished.'

"Another man lost his ring and came to me in a panic. He didn't care what it cost, he wanted a replacement!

"I knew what he meant. Before I got my 15-year ring, I would have been with those employees who preferred cash. But now I wouldn't trade it for the world."

Many companies agree. "Dollars and cents are not where it's at in tenure recognition," says Marilyn K. Williams of Bowers Worldwide Travel Management, a company that uses jewelry or stationery/desk items, as well as travel packages, to reward the "loyalty, honesty and long-term relationships that our employees expect as much from us as we do from them."

Rather than specify five-, 10- or 15-year recognition awards, Bowers offers its employees a choice. "Some people like to have the jewelry items as day-in/day-out reminders to themselves and others of their 'pride in ownership' in their company and work, while others prefer the travel packages," says Bowers. "It's not just the photographs and memories that they bring back from their trips, but the ongoing relationships they forged with people—now friends—they met during their travels."

Cash awards for some kind of bonuses are appropriate, she adds, but a recognition that resonates with "thanks for a job well done" over the months and years after it is given "works better for our employees."

What Kind of Awards Should You Give?

Most businesses can benefit from recognizing loyalty among workers. But what other types of awards will motivate employees and help your business reach its goals?

Answering this question may require some soul searching on your part.

Clearly, some types of award programs can actually undermine the company's long-term goals. For instance, if you offer an award to the salesperson who brings in the most *new* business during a particular month, you actually may be encouraging your sales staff to ignore existing accounts—at least until the contest ends. Since repeat business is vital to any organization, this kind of behavior obviously would be detrimental to the company over the long haul.

In other words, when creating an awards program, it is vital that you take care to reward the specific behavior you desire.

The Pontiac Master Sales Guild does this among car salespeople (a group that isn't exactly known for demonstrating the kind of behavior most business people would desire). For more than 40 years now, the guild has been honoring Pontiac salespeople and sales managers for outstanding performance not only in the area of sales, but also in the areas of product knowledge and customer satisfaction.

A similar award is given by Blue Ridge Best Foods Inc. for the District Manager of the Year in Virginia and West Virginia. Jonathan Secrist, district manager of the Omelet Shoppe restaurants in Salem and Princeton, West Virginia, took the title for the third consecutive year in 1996, after tallying the biggest gains in sales and the best cost savings at his locations. The company also considers phone bills, awarding points to district managers on a monthly basis. The winner, who receives a trip to Las Vegas, is announced at a large awards banquet that is attended by all the district managers, corporate management and officers, and their wives.

Companies increasingly are trying to tie compensation to performance these days. And this is leading to more and more cash-incentive and performance-based-pay programs.

Should Money Be Part—or All—of the Award?

According to a 1996 poll of 1,681 businesses nationwide conducted by Hewitt Associates, 61 percent reported using bonuses and other "variable compensation" to pay their employees.

Of the 61 percent of companies that offered variable pay rewards, the most common type of rewards were:

Special recognition awards	51%
Individual performance awards	44%
Business incentives	43%
Cash profit-sharing	29%

However, the jury is still out on whether many of these performance-based-pay programs actually improve employees' performance—especially at very large companies where bonuses are linked almost exclusively to the bottom line of the entire business.

For instance, in the banking field, analysts question whether these compensation programs even have anything to do with employees' performance. "In a world where Alan Greenspan is having a great day with interest rates and the stock market is going up and up, there's really a sort of feeling of windfall about these programs," David Berry, a banking analyst with Keefe, Bruyette & Woods, told *American Banker*. "You could have mediocre performance and people could still make a lot of money.

"What you'd really like to do is isolate relative performance, according to some index," he added. "Then you would not be rewarding people for things that are clearly external to them—but for their actual decisions."

Because compensation rewards generally are mishandled, they typically mean little more to an employee than inflation indexing or a partial payback for the value he or she added to the company through hard work and initiative. Therefore, when a company gives awards in the form of pay increases or bonuses, they are perceived as an entitlement, rather than a pat on the back for a job well done.

There are four main problems with compensation-oriented awards:

- **They do not flow from the business process.** "Compensation plan designers must understand the customer chain, the work process, and how and where employees add value," according to an article by Theodore R. Buyniski in *Compensation and Benefits Review*. "When plan designers do not understand these elements, the result is a plan that treats all employees similarly or that is based on what everyone else is doing. In the short run, this may still work ... [but] over time, [it] will become a source of competitive disadvantage as the company fails to maximize its return on its investment in human capital."

- **They do not link the employee with the action**. If there is no clear link between how employees create—or destroy—value (i.e., between the actions of a soda truck driver and the price of the soda company's stock), compensation rewards will make no sense to the employee.

- **They do not provide sufficient reward opportunity**. The amount of a company's value surplus that is "shared" via compensation awards is no more or less than that which will "encourage employees to create additional value." Unfortunately, this fundamental concept of compensation rewards is generally so misunderstood by employees that its rewards are seen by them as nothing more than entitlements.

- **They are not timely**. "Since feedback means more when it closely follows an action," Buyniski adds, "feedback pay should follow results as soon as they become measurable, with a minimum of administrative delay."

Once you have recognized the common problems associated with bonus/compensation programs, it is possible to design financial awards as part of a special recognition program. This way, you can make sure those awards are tied to the specific type of performance you desire.

Cash awards are prevalent in business today, according to a recent Towers Perrin survey of 750 U.S. corporations, which found that more than half of these companies have some sort of recognition program in place. However, respondents felt that public recognition is a good way to create role models for other workers.

The Timken bearing and steel company in Canton, Ohio, is one of a growing number of businesses that has decided to trade in its cash-for-suggestions program in favor of a nonmonetary Dedication to Excellence Award. Lloyd Groves, manager of associate services, explained the reason for the switch: "A lot of the time, it was centered on monetary values," he said. "It recognized people as being independent rather than working in teams."

Groves believes the suggestion program was rewarding people with cash when they actually were seeking recognition.

"We were rewarding behavior that was non-beneficial to the company—and, ultimately, the employees themselves," said Groves. "Giving monetary awards for money-saving innovations made sense on the surface, but it served to erode the kind of total quality management program we wanted for Timken.

"People would horde ideas in order to maximize their personal profit from the cash awards they might receive for them. And why not, when our awards program was structured to encourage exactly that kind of behavior?

Chapter 2—Using Awards Within Your Business

"By shifting over to a recognition program that emphasized quality rather than quantity, we moved to the right track. For example, our Latrobe subsidiary got a special steel order late one afternoon for the material needed in an artificial heart valve. The plant had the order on a truck in an hour, and the letter they later received from the heart-surgery survivor praising their efforts meant more to them than any cash award."

It's not always easy to decide whether to give cash, gift certificates, vacations, prizes, plaques or statuettes to your employees. In many cases, the best bet may be to ask your employees what they want. After all, they alone know what truly motivates them.

Enhancing Your Business's Image

An in-house awards program not only motivates employees and rewards the kind of behavior you desire. It also can lead to outside recognition, enhancing your business's image in the community and its industry—and with customers.

For example, safety is a big concern for J. Frank Schmidt & Son Co., Oregon's largest grower of shade and ornamental trees. The company has been able to reach its goals for a safe working environment by involving employees in the process.

Jeanette Hubbard, chairwoman of the Association of Oregon Nurserymen's safety committee, points out that Schmidt works extra hard to include employees in developing ways to prevent on-the-job injuries. Then, to recognize workers and their families, the company holds a safety awards fiesta each year.

"They do an excellent job of instilling the need for

safety and then rewarding workers for it," Hubbard said.

The awards program obviously has paid off for workers by reducing injuries. It also has paid off for the company by cutting workers' compensation insurance costs.

In addition, the internal awards program has led to recognition by the company's peer group. In 1996, the Association of Oregon Nurserymen gave Schmidt its annual safety award.

The association award, in turn, led to increased customer awareness of the firm, thanks to writeups in local newspapers.

Fluor Daniel, a Southern California company involved in engineering, construction, maintenance and operation of production plants, as well as corporate consulting, has seen similar positive results from its employee awards program.

Greg Meyer, the manager of Fluor Daniel's Chicago office, passed out some 150 Most Valuable Player (MVP) awards during the company's 1996 fiscal year— to employees who came up with time- and money-saving proposals. The MVP awards include both public recognition and a cash prize.

The public part comes at the office's annual Christmas breakfast for the entire staff of more than 400— which, in 1996, was served by managers dressed in aprons and Santa hats. Meyer says the annual event reflects his company's goal to make the work environment friendlier—and thus produce a more successful company.

"We try to foster good communication and we listen to employees' ideas," said Meyer. "We give employees the training, tools, authority and the feedback for them to take action and get things done."

In one case, employees' ideas saved the company—and its client—substantial time and money. According to Meyer, the company had been hired to partially demolish and reconstruct an older building, but the architectural drawings of the structure had been lost. In this sort of situation, the company ordinarily would redraw the entire building, floor by floor, which could take weeks or even months.

"Instead," said Meyer, "our employees suggested we take photographs of the inside of the building and transfer them to computers, then use those photos in place of the drawings."

The company had to buy digital cameras and the appropriate computer software. But the relatively minor expense paid off substantially in time and man-hours saved. Plus, construction workers were much happier to be working from photos, rather than abstract drawings.

"It was great. It saved us and our client a lot of money and virtually everyone loved it," Meyer said proudly. "They [the employees] put all the pieces together to make it work. I just helped them get it done."

Involving and empowering employees in this way—and rewarding them for their efforts—has paid off nicely for Fluor Daniel, especially on the bottom line. It has even garnered the company the attention and respect of its peers: Based primarily on revenue volume, the firm was ranked first among the nation's Top 400 Contractors in 1996 and fourth among the Top 500 Design Firms by *Engineering News-Record*, an industry publication.

Getting the Most Out of an Awards Program

"Sometimes money isn't all people work for," said John Cochran, chief executive of FirstMerit, a bank based in Akron, Ohio. While Cochran points out that recognition should not be a substitute for fair pay, his company launched a new employee recognition campaign in 1996 to create role models and recognize employees who outperformed expectations.

That year, more than 200 FirstMerit employees and their guests were honored at a huge tent party outside the Rock and Roll Hall of Fame and Museum—as the culmination of the first year of the bank's FirstHonors program. The event included dinner, dancing and private access to the museum.

"If there are certain values you have in a company—like customer service and employee morale—that has to get transmitted some way, and this is the way to do it," said Cochran.

To qualify for an invite to the party, the company established two different sets of criteria. People in sales-oriented positions, including loan officers, bank managers and private banking managers, had to meet certain financial goals. Employees in other areas, including secretarial and support staffs, tellers and operations people, were nominated by their peers and supervisors throughout the year.

To notify the winners, FirstMerit executives showed up at the branch offices to deliver bouquets of balloons, each of which was anchored by an invitation to the gala event. The winners also received a FirstMerit T-shirt, which was the mandatory attire for the big bash.

The FirstHonors program is a good example of rewarding the type of behavior a company desires—

and getting a lot of mileage out of a single awards program.

The program is building momentum, too. As Dixie Vinez of First Merit points out, "Now people are working really hard because they want to go to the next event. It's having a very positive impact."

3 Giving Awards to Other Companies

There are a number of reasons to give out awards to other companies. And virtually all of them have benefits for your business.

For instance, you may want to set up an awards program to recognize suppliers whose products always arrive on time or early, or who regularly provide goods or services at a quality better than the norm—once again, distinguishing the extraordinary from the ordinary. Much like in-house awards, these supplier awards would encourage the sort of behavior your company desires.

For example, Abbott Laboratories has been giving out Preferred Supplier and Outstanding Performer awards each year since 1994. The company uses a quarterly grading system to determine who will receive the awards, for on-time delivery, prompt technical service, cost-reduction recommendations, overall quality and 14 other categories.

Or you might set up a program to recognize businesses that use the products your company sells or manufactures. For example, Microsoft Corp. gives out the Leonardo Awards, which, according to the software giant, "highlight manufacturing system solutions whose benefits don't stop at the bottom line." The basic eligibility requirement is that candidates have used Microsoft software to gain competitive advantages through increased efficiency.

The Golden Mouse Awards are similar to the Leonardo Awards, insofar as they are given by a software manufacturer (Intergraph Corp.) for art produced with Intergraph-supported software. Unlike most business awards, they are not given at a trade show or industry conference, but at an annual meeting of the International Intergraph Graphics Users Group (IGUG) at the corporation's headquarters in Alabama. In effect, they are a hybrid of business and association awards (discussed in Chapter 4), with the product customers comprising the membership of the association (IGUG).

These sorts of awards encourage people to buy and use your product regularly—to develop the necessary expertise to qualify for the competition. And the more high-caliber people you can attract to your product, the better—especially when it comes time to publicize your awards program. (For more on how to take advantage of opportunities for publicity, see Chapter 14.)

Magazine Awards

Magazines frequently give out business awards, as well. At the COMDEX/Fall 1995 computer trade show, Microsoft received awards from *PC Magazine*, *PC/Computing*, *PC Laptop Computers Magazine* and *Computer Retail Week*.

Three weeks later, Microsoft received 10 more awards from *DBMS* magazine.

In January of 1995, it won *BYTE* and *Data Communications* awards.

In 1994, just from publications not mentioned above, it won awards from *Network Computing, Information Week, Software Digest, Data Based Advisor, Info World, LAN Magazine, Windows Magazine, NetWare Solutions Magazine, Communications Week* and *Network Computing*.

The business benefit of these magazine awards also goes to the presenter. When the publisher and editor-in-chief of *BYTE Magazine* presents an award at a major trade show or industry convention, the magazine is positioning itself as more than just a "biz zine" servicing the industry as a niche publication. Now it can portray itself as the formulator of a "distinctive global agenda for collecting, analyzing and presenting technology information for computing experts."

By analyzing the comparative usefulness of systems, portable computers, applications software, development software, Internet products and other tools of the digital domain, *BYTE* identifies "hardware and software that could have a strong influence on computing." Through its awards, *BYTE* helps the industry sort through the mass of available products and cull the utile from the clunkers.

In addition, many of the companies whose products receive awards will go on to list those awards in advertisements. This is a tremendous boon to the award-giver. For instance, a *BYTE* award recipient might go on to mention the award—and *BYTE Magazine*'s name—in ads over the course of the next year. And those ads surely will appear in magazines that compete with *BYTE*—positioning *BYTE* as an authority in readers' eyes and getting *BYTE* some free advertising (in venues in which it probably would not be able to advertise on its own, either).

Many magazines further capitalize on awards as a source of publicity by offering winners display pieces that they can take to trade shows—getting the magazine additional exposure among showgoers at a minimal cost.

Marketing Exposure

By playing up the marketing exposure benefits of awards, you can encourage more companies to compete for an award you offer.

For instance, the Software Publishers Association's (SPA's) Codie Awards (for excellence in game, consumer, business/home office, school and other computer software) provide a textbook example of how to promote your awards program—and how to convey the value of this promotion to entrants.

SPA advertises that contestants will receive the following types of exposure:

- Attention from national and trade journalists: "In the preliminary judging phase, your product will be viewed and critiqued by leading software trade journalists, national technology writers, teachers and state technology education specialists."

- On-line presence: "A special 'nominee' designation will be displayed beside your company's entry in SPA's software industry directory."

- On-line promotion and the World Wide Web title showcase: "Specific product information displayed with a link to your home page, product reviews, as well as traditional and on-line retailers."

- Consumer traffic: During the final balloting process, means will be taken to link the software with retailers and dealers, which will "strengthen the bond between the Codie Awards and retail chains and gain consumer awareness for all finalists and winners."

- Showcasing product to potential business partners: Finalists will have the opportunity to get their product in the hands of all voting members for their consideration prior to their vote.

- Promotion of finalists: "All Codie Award finalists will be provided with a 'finalist' logo available for use on all promotional materials and/or retail boxes. SPA will also promote your finalist product through nationwide press releases, links to finalist companies from SPA's web site, feature articles in SPA's magazine *Upgrade* and demonstrations at trade shows before and after the Codie Awards ceremony."

- Promotion of winners: "SPA will promote your Codie Award-winning title through editorial coverage, nationwide press releases and a full public relations campaign leading up to and following the event. Winners receive a display in the Winners Showcase located on SPA's web site throughout 1997.

In addition, an informational brochure distributed to thousands of industry professionals at trade shows and conferences will feature all winning titles. A 'winner' logo is also supplied to all winning titles for use on promotional materials, including retail boxes."

Similarly, the Alliance for Community Media promotes its Hometown Video Festival as an opportunity for "winners [to] receive national visibility!" Not only will each recipient be announced and honored at the Milwaukee awards presentation with an engraved plaque, but the Alliance will:

- nationally distribute winning videos;

- give the winners complimentary admission to its international conference and trade show; and

- list the winners in its membership journal, winners directory and festival catalog.

Using Awards to Boost Sales

A variation on the magazine business award is what is known in the trade as the "annual franchise feature." Much like *Sports Illustrated*'s swimsuit issue (which brings in more than $20 million in advertising and boosts sales by 2 million copies) or *Seventeen*'s prom special (which generated additional sales of 228,000 copies in 1995), these annual features use awards and recognition to sell magazines.

Some examples:

- *Gentlemen's Quarterly*'s "Men of the Year." The November 1996 issue had 410 pages of advertising and sold 400,000 copies—making it the biggest and most profitable *GQ* in five years.

- *Time*'s "Man of the Year." The 1996 award issue was expected to bring in about $17 million in advertising, doubling the weekly average.

- *People*'s "25 Most Intriguing People of the Year." This is always the biggest issue of the year, with 2 million copies on newsstands.

- *Esquire*'s "Dubious Achievement Awards." The January 1995 awards issue outsold the year's next best-selling issue by 15 percent.

Survey Says ...

Some business awards are based on market surveys. One firm involved in this sort of awards program is J.D. Power and Associates. You've probably heard of this international marketing information company— since it often gets mentioned in car makers' ads on TV and in print.

One of the surveys Power conducts is the APEAL study of Automotive Performance, Execution and Layout, in which the firm "asks new vehicle owners to rate their vehicles on more than 100 attributes, [and the responses are] designed to identify what owners really like about their new car or truck," according to the company. "The APEAL study is based on responses from more than 25,000 new car and truck owners after three months of ownership. It is the only study that exclusively measures owners' feelings about their new cars and trucks."

It addresses eight aspects of the vehicle, and quantifies what owners like and why. These eight elements are:

- vehicle styling;

- engine and transmission;

- comfort and convenience;

- ride and handling;

- seats;

- heating, ventilation and cooling;

- cockpit and instrument panel; and

- sound system.

Says Power, "When the findings of this study are examined in detail—across vehicle segments—it provides designers, engineers, brand managers and product planners with considerable insight into what helps differentiate one vehicle from another."

It also provides the winners with a chance to publicize the results.

Whenever the winners of a survey are announced—particularly one of Power's quality surveys—you can expect magazines and newspapers to carry articles detailing the results. And you can expect the winning companies to spread the word through advertising.

Naturally, all of this publicity mentions J.D. Power's name, which only helps build the firm's consulting and market research business.

Promoting Values

Business awards also can be given for the encouragement and promotion of societal values.

For example, the Dove Foundation's Dove Seal is

awarded to home videos—primarily movies—rated "family-friendly" by its film review board. The review board includes an advisory adjunct of many nationally known individuals, including Steve Allen (comedian, author, composer), Dean Jones (actor, producer), Tom Landry (former head coach of the Dallas Cowboys), Michael Medved (author and film critic) and Joe Paterno (head coach at Penn State University).

The purpose of the Dove Seal is to make it easy for customers to identify titles that are free of audio and visual offenses to children. Steve Allen calls it "the Good Housekeeping Seal for family entertainment."

More than 1,500 videos have been awarded the Dove Seal, and the foundation is expanding its review process to include video games and web sites on the Internet.

Finding Your Way Through the Clutter

The Dove Seal is a fine example of an award that helps consumers find their way through a barrage of products or services. The Good Housekeeping Seal of Approval, awarded by *Good Housekeeping* magazine, is another such example.

So are the *Newsweek* Editor's Choice awards. The magazine gave out 50 Editor's Choice awards in 1996 for best children's CD-ROM products—after considering more than 400 candidates. One of the winners was GO WEST!

A simulation program, GO WEST! acquaints students with homesteading issues, such as how to build a house and where to plant the crops. In order to make decisions, they must gather and weigh information from newspapers, catalogs and advice from townspeople and other neighbors about current events and farming. Students take the information beyond the simulations and into discussions related to society, science and economy of the past and present.

"GO WEST! is one of the outstanding multimedia CD-ROM products available for children," said Michael Rogers, contributing editor of *Newsweek* and executive producer of the *Newsweek* Parent's Guide to Children's Software 97 web site. "By recognizing children's software products that are entertaining, informative and educational, we are providing parents with an objective guide to make sense of the maze of titles on the market today."

In judging the products for the *Newsweek* award, the magazine editors, parents, children and educators from across the country were guided by strict criteria, including how well the product makes use of multimedia, encourages decision-making, gives consistent feedback, provides multiple layers of sophistication, requires interactivity, and allows for self-paced learning and exploration.

Information on GO WEST! appeared on *Newsweek*'s web site, and also was featured in *Newsweek*'s Fall/Winter 1996 *Computers & Family* magazine.

Products that receive a *Newsweek* Editor's Choice award in one of the six categories (creativity, learning, problem solving, reading, adventure and reference) then become eligible for the annual "Best Of" award—making the Editor's Choice not just an awards program, but also a nominating process. (This is a good way to make nominees feel like winners, too.)

The Internet is another area that contains a barrage of products—web sites, in this case. It was estimated that there were already more than 900,000 in existence at the beginning of 1997. Fortunately, a number of companies have decided to offer awards programs for web sites to help net surfers find the gems and navigate around the duds.

For example, the InfiNet Co. of Norfolk, Virginia, an Internet access provider, sponsors the "Cool Site of the Day" as a service to web users. InfiNet checks out 200 sites each day in search of the coolest one. Reported the *Los Angeles Times*:

> Getting around the web is relatively easy if you know your destination, because every web page has an address, or URL, that begins with the code "http://". But if you want to do research, or just poke around the most interesting sites, you need guidance, just like a telephone caller who doesn't have the number.
>
> As one cool-site arbiter summed up the job of people who make their living selecting and awarding cutting edge/exciting/new/cool web sites: "We waste our time so you don't have to."

"Site of the Week" and Proud Eagle Awards (in recognition of web sites that promote racial harmony) are among the many awards given to Internet users. But even though these awards exist only as digital bytes manifested on computer screens, they fulfill the general purpose of awards by identifying the extraordinary within the mass of the ordinary. This is becoming especially important on the vast web of the

Internet, as one Proud Eagle winner explained:

> I go to a search engine and look for a key word about a topic that interests me. I may get thousands of related sites. Some are tagged as award-winners. I go to them first. Wouldn't you?

Award Overload

You probably would, unless you had grown cynical about the ubiquity of web awards. The *Wall Street Journal* reports that many Net users blame the proliferation of little awards for devaluing the entire concept. It even quotes one web surfer as saying, "Most of the people handing out awards are just trying to drive traffic back to their site. ... It's purely a hit-driving mechanism."

This is because the trophies displayed at winning sites typically are "hot linked" back to the address that issued the awards. "Hence a web watcher checking out the Firewalking Homepage," says the *Journal*, "would see its Cosmic Site of the Night Award, a blue-and-gold badge. Clicking on the badge would transport the user to the home page of AdZe MiXXe, an astrologer in West Chester, Pennsylvania, who offers daily horoscopes and encourages users to order customized readings for $24 to $150.

"Consultants who advise web sites on how to generate traffic routinely recommend awards-fishing as an effective tactic. It isn't difficult: At most awards sites, simply stopping by and dropping off an electronic note of self-nomination is enough to place your site in consideration."

The question is: Who is giving out these awards? And what are the criteria for winning? Dana Groulx, who oversees the web site of the Tampa Bay, Florida, chapter of Mensa, told the *Journal*, "I'm not going to waste my time submitting stuff for these things. The Top 5% award—I mean, according to whom?"

Clearly, an explosion of awards—many of which are given for little more than self-promotion—can devalue the entire awards process. But experienced web surfers still will be familiar with the more useful (and credible) Internet awards and probably still will skip to those award-winning sites.

The key when you are setting up a business-to-business awards program is to create an award that has meaning. You need to establish relevant criteria, and create an award that actually provides a service—not only in terms of promoting your company, but in terms of recognizing true excellence and helping promote the recipient company. Only by doing this are you truly helping consumers sort through all the clutter in their search for quality products and services.

4

Association Awards

Over the years, individuals and businesses typically join numerous associations. You may be a member of one or more professional societies or guilds, and your company may be a member of any number of trade groups. You also may be affiliated with a union.

If you are involved in several associations, that makes you a typical American, at least according to Alexis de Tocqueville. He wrote about Americans' propensity for creating and joining associations of all types back in 1835, in *Democracy in America*:

> Americans of all ages, all conditions, and all dispositions constantly form associations. They have not only commercial and manufacturing companies, in which all take part, but associations of a thousand other kinds, religious, moral, serious, futile, general or restricted, enormous or diminutive. The Americans make associations to give entertainments, to found seminaries, to build inns, to construct churches, to diffuse books, to send missionaries to the antipodes; in this manner they found hospitals, prisons, and schools. If it is proposed to inculcate some truth or to foster some feeling by the encouragement of a great example, they form a society.

Today, the *ultimate* goal of a trade association is increased income from its product or service. But the goals of professional societies are commonly considered to point more toward the expansion of knowledge or the establishment of professional standards.

Because they set standards of excellence, it should not be surprising that many associations have chosen to give awards to members—and often even to non-members.

Your company may want to enter the competition for one or more of these awards. Or if you belong to an association that does not yet have an awards program in place, you may want to take the initiative and begin one.

Whether you're going to be on the giving or the receiving end of association awards, it's important to remember that these types of awards have two common characteristics:

1) They represent the professional purpose of their parent association.

2) Their intent is to further the goals of the association and reflect its values.

Furthering the Group's Mission

An association's mission statement should provide the context for its awards.

For example, according to the Environmental Media Association's call for entries to its award program in 1996, that group's stated purpose is "to mobilize the entertainment community in a global effort to educate people about environmental problems and inspire them to act on those problems now." Therefore, its awards "recognize film, television and music productions which increase public awareness of environmental problems and inspire personal action on these problems."

The call for entries asks:

> What makes a work environmental? Sometimes it can be as simple as a single beat in a half-hour television comedy. It can also be as complex as the theme for an entire feature film. It may even be the conditions under which the work was made (as with the *Alternative N.R.G.* album, which was produced with solar energy). As long as the work clearly delivers an environmental message in some way ...

The American National Standards Institute (ANSI) has as its primary goal the "enhancement of global competitiveness of U.S. business and the American quality of life by promoting and facilitating voluntary consensus standards and conformity assessment systems and promoting their integrity." The ANSI awards program, therefore, is designed to "recognize business and standards community leaders who have made significant contributions to national and international standardization." The institute has awards categories for "advancing information technology standards" and "advancing standardization as a management tool."

The National Institute of Packaging, Handling and Logistics Engineers (NIPHLE) is dedicated to solving logistics problems through proper packaging and handling design. This institute serves government and industry specialists by facilitating the exchange of information—to encourage improvements in design, materials, equipment, application, standardization and cost evaluation methods that will facilitate logistics planning.

To further its goals, the Institute has created three awards programs. First, it provides recognition to notable individuals with its Annual Achievement Awards and to firms or agencies with its Distinguished Service Awards. The awards are based on the nominee's total contribution to the field, rather than to a particular project or during a particular period of time—and membership in the Institute is not a prerequisite for winning. The John C. Wilford Memorial Award for outstanding contributions to the field of packaging, on the other hand, is open only to NIPHLE members. In addition, NIPHLE sponsors an annual packaging, handling and logistics design competition.

To further its educational goals, the NIPHLE set up a scholarship program. However, an association also can create an awards variation known as a "challenge" to further educational goals. For example, in 1995, the Direct Marketing Association set up the DMA Environmental Stewardship Challenge to encourage its members to assess and improve their waste-management practices. "By taking the challenge," the organization stated, "many direct marketers will find they can achieve significant cost savings while increasing recycling and reducing the waste associated with their operations."

In this case, the challenge is the competition. The awards are good environmental stewardship and increased profits.

One of the best-known association awards is the Primetime Emmy Award, which is given by the Academy of Television Arts & Sciences. The story of how the Academy began and how the Emmys helped it flourish exemplifies the two common characteristics of association awards—and may help you launch your own association's awards program.

The Academy of Television Arts & Sciences was originated in 1946 as a discussion group for a small set of people who were working in the new medium. There was a lot to discuss:

- what would be shown on television;

- how to improve the technical quality of the recording and transmission of the television image;

- how to build and expand the new medium.

Beginning as a practical forum for the exchange of views on scientific, aesthetic, financial and legal topics, the Academy was composed of a group of television pioneers who initially got together to bring some collegiality and social interaction to the semi-isolation of their commercially marginal, relatively experimental business.

Because they were in the television business, they talked about picture tubes, transmission lines, studio audiences, selling to sponsors, the effect of hot lights on makeup, the possibility of getting established radio stars to appear on their shows and a host of other issues pertinent to 1946 television in Los Angeles.

Within two years of its inception, the little discussion group saw the possibility of developing standards of excellence for television programming—and offering awards based on them.

The members knew that awards could be used to recognize outstanding achievement in their burgeoning industry. After all, the Motion Picture Academy had been rewarding excellence in movies since the 1920s with its Oscar, so why couldn't the TV Academy begin rewarding excellence in television with its own award, the Emmy? (Emmy is a feminization of "Immy," engineering slang for the image orthicon tube, an early picture tube. Legend has it that Oscar got his name because he looked like Betty Davis' husband, Oscar. Another story has it that Academy librarian Margaret Herrick thought it resembled her Uncle Oscar. Whatever the true origins of the nickname, its official name is the Academy Award of Merit.)

To do great things, Emmy had to have a great look. Like Oscar, she needed a shiny gold plate and a metaphoric base—Oscar stood on a film reel, Emmy on a global grid—but that was where the comparison stopped. Unlike the art deco sentry of the Motion Picture Academy, Emmy appeared as a lithe, art nouveau muse of art who exalted the electron of science. In this one image, her designer (Louis McManus) created a beautiful statuette and a personification of the Academy's aim, "to further the arts and sciences of television."

The Emmys were first awarded at the Hollywood Athletic Club on January 25, 1949. The first five Emmys went to the most popular television program (Pantomime Quiz), best film made for television (The Necklace) and most outstanding TV personality (Shirley Dinsdale and her puppet Judy Splinters).

There was also a technical award for a "phasefinder" and a station award that went to Los Angeles broadcast pioneer KTLA.

Might little Emmy grow up like Cousin Oscar, who had brought so much recognition to the family of motion pictures? If Oscar could bring standing and prestige to the movies, couldn't Emmy could do the same for television?

If so, the awards truly would represent the professional purpose of their parent association, further the goals of the association and reflect its values.

The importance of association awards generally is tied to the importance and stability of the association.

For instance, the Society of Plastics Engineers (SPE), an international nonprofit group with 38,000 members, has been around since 1942. Its Automotive Division has been giving awards for 26 years. Clearly, this is a stable organization—and according to Jay Braboy, the 1996 awards banquet's publicity chairman, the awards are considered "the Grammy of the plastics industry."

The importance of the SPE awards was reflected in the number and caliber of people who attended the awards banquet—more than 1,000 top automotive executives, engineers and suppliers, as well as members of the media—and in the number and caliber of entries.

In 1996, 80 to 120 parts were nominated for the Most Innovative Use of Plastics Award in the categories of body interior, body exterior, chassis/hardware, powertrain, material, process, environmental and Hall of Fame. They were judged based on the trend-setting

Important Association, Important Awards

nature of the plastics application and its impact on the auto industry, as well as innovations in design, engineering, manufacture, assembly, parts integration, and weight and cost reduction. The nomination voted best overall would receive the Grand Award.

Judging for this award is done in two stages. The association's Automotive Division Board of Directors votes to choose the finalists. Then a Blue Ribbon Panel of trade publication editors and industry experts determines the winners, which are announced at an awards banquet.

The winners in 1995 included Donnelly Corp. in the body exterior category, for its single-sided encapsulated glazing process for the 1996 Chrysler Corp. minivans; Venture Industries in the process category, for its interior trim package for the 1996 GMC Savana and Chevy Express; and BASF Corp. in the environmental category, for its coextruded plastic fuel tank for the 1996 Chrysler Jeep Grand Cherokee. In addition, Autodie International Inc. won the award for the chassis/hardware category, as well as the Grand Award, for the integrated front end system on the 1996 Ford Taurus and Mercury Sable. And GM Delphi's Guideflex bumper energy absorber, which was first used on the 1974 Chevrolet Corvette, netted the company an induction into the Hall of Fame.

Depreciating an Award

Because the importance of association awards is tied to the importance and stability of the association, when associations fracture and dissidents set up competing awards, an association's awards can suffer.

As an example, in 1977, the Television Academy

was split with dissension on the issue of which members could vote for which categories, with the dissident faction insisting that only legitimate peers of the actors, writers, directors and other Emmy entrants were qualified to vote for them (rather than any member of the Academy). The matter was resolved in court, when the Academy was split into two separate academies.

The "divorce" produced an Academy in Los Angeles (with "custody" of the Primetime and Los Angeles-area Emmy competitions) and the National Academy in New York (with "custody" of all other national and regional competitions). As with most divorces, the "children" suffered from the loss of a coherent, functional set of "parents."

A more recent example of association strife and awards fallout involves the Hollywood Foreign Press Association (HFPA), which administers the Golden Globe Awards. In 1994, the HFPA suspended its then-president, Mirjana van Blaricom, following a "bylaws dispute." Two years later, the ex-president formed the International Press Academy (IPA) and announced that the group would put on its own awards program (the Golden Satellites), which would be presented just days before the Golden Globes held its nationally televised awards show.

The goal of the new association, van Blaricom told the *Los Angeles Times*, was "to create a more open, broader-based, 'less easily manipulated' operation than the HFPA, which has 85 Los Angeles-based members who write for foreign publications ... many of whom 'are car dealers, accountants—only part-time journalists whom Hollywood caters to because they give out awards. The industry is kept hostage by those little Golden Globes.' "

According to the trade paper the *Hollywood Reporter*, the HFPA "did not consider a new [foreign press] organization a threat."

And although van Blaricom claimed the IPA was "not competing with them," she told the *Times* that "if the business is serious, they'll recognize us in the end."

"Entertainment is the great American export and Hollywood deserves better," she said. "I respect the People's Choice Awards more than the Globes—at least they don't pretend to be something they're not."

Clearly, the fighting between the two groups did little to improve the image of either association—or its awards. After all the back and forth between the HFPA and the IPA, the *Reporter*'s headline most succinctly summarized the situation: "Spinoff Group Circles Globes."

Peer Recognition

In spite of her less-than-diplomatic approach, van Blaricom did recognize one of the best parts of association awards: the fact that they represent recognition by one's peers—the people who are most likely to understand just how much you or your business have gone through to get where you are today.

For instance, the American Physical Society is a membership association closely linked to the development of the technology that gave the world the Internet. This group of distinguished physicists confirms the sense of the importance and utility of awards in its description of them as a symbol "of the admiration of a physicist's peers." The society adds that each award "demonstrates that the recipient's accomplishments and contributions to physics are judged exceptional by those of his colleagues who are best able to judge their value."

Physicists-in-training are some of the competitors in Cal Tech's Engineering Design Contest. In this variation on association awards (the school being the "association," the awards being held for the purpose of furthering the educational goals of the association), "students control what are essentially homemade toy cars via joysticks. To win, your device must scoop up golf balls and ferry them into the drain faster than anyone else's. But, as in other sports, the best defense is a good offense—so you must also ram, trap or block your enemy by any means necessary. ... The winner gets a trophy adorned with a giant gear."

The Pioneer Award, which is presented each year at the MultiUnit Foodservice Operators (MUFSO) conference, honors a veteran for dedication and contribution to the food service industry. In 1996, that honor went to Leon "Pete" Harman, who became the first Kentucky Fried Chicken franchisee in 1952, when he began serving chicken made from Col. Harland Sanders' secret recipe at his restaurant in Salt Lake City. Harman Management Co. has since opened more than 350 restaurants in the United States, making it KFC's largest privately held franchisee.

Harman's company is credited with coining the "Kentucky Fried Chicken" brand name and developing the marketing phrase "finger-lickin' good." The Pioneer Award recognized Harman's contributions in helping build the Kentucky Fried Chicken brand—

and the fact that he never complained when the attention was focused on Sanders, the concept's founder and spokesperson.

Harman also was said to have developed the first bundled meal in 1957, when he packaged 14 pieces of chicken, mashed potatoes, biscuits and gravy for $3.50. And he was a founding member of the Utah Restaurant Association. He also created one of the first employee-ownership programs, which gives restaurant managers equity in their stores today.

During a video that accompanied the award presentation, Harman's colleagues repeatedly pointed out that he was long overdue to receive the Pioneer award, according to *Nation's Restaurant News*.

The recognition of his peers clearly touched Harman. "This is the highest award that I have ever received, and I've been given a lot of awards in my life," he said, adding that his most valuable ideas and lessons came from his employees. "Five thousand employees bought the ticket for me to be here tonight."

The American Tree Farm System (ATFS) is another group that provides valuable peer recognition via its National Tree Farmer of the Year award. The winners in 1996, Rachel and Don Jordan from Wisconsin, were chosen from among 70,000 registered tree farmers. Criteria range from harvest quality to forest management practices.

The Jordans farm oak, walnut, ash, hickory, cherry and other deciduous trees, which are used for everything from railroad ties to fine furniture. Harvests are whenever the trees are ready. Since 1982, the Jordans have harvested 1.8 million board feet of saw timber, as well as 225 poles and 380 cords of firewood.

But quantity doesn't always equate with quality, especially when it comes to tree farming. And the award is designed to reward environmentally sound practices. "The Jordans' harvests have dramatically increased wildlife habitat," said Joel Aanensen, chairman of the Wisconsin Tree Farm Committee. "Deer, grouse and turkey numbers have soared. Many old trees with hollow cavities have been left standing for use by nesting birds and animals."

Winning national recognition from their peers has brought the Jordans international attention, as well. According to the *Wisconsin State Journal*, "Tree farmers from Europe have visited the Jordan farm to study their environmental management."

For Members Only

While the Emmys are given without regard to whether the recipients are members of the Academy, many association awards are for members only. Two examples:

- The Vinyl Window and Door Institute Awards for Outstanding Performance are given only to projects using vinyl windows and doors supplied by members of the institute.

- The Marconi Radio Awards, which are given by the National Association of Broadcasters, recognize the NAB member Station of the Year, NAB member Network/Syndicated Personality of the Year, etc. (In addition to its members-only awards, the NAB gives Crystal Radio Awards, which recognize excellence in community service to NAB or non-NAB subscribers.)

The Lydia Awards also are limited to a select membership—an Internet "news group" of body art (tattooing and body piercing) subjects. The Lydias (after the song lyrics about "Lydia the Tattooed Lady") are acrylic statuettes given at an annual dinner attended by group members. Among the categories is "Wittiest Responses to People Who Go Out of Their Way to Criticize the Body Art of Total Strangers Minding Their Own Business and Bothering No One."

Vendor Recognition

Numerous associations have set up awards programs to recognize their vendors, who also may be associate or adjunct members. Again, these awards give an association a chance to reward the type of behavior it desires. Winning one of these awards also can translate into more business for the vendor, which makes the award good business on both ends.

An example is the American Association of Respiratory Care's annual award for outstanding work by manufacturers in the field of respiratory care. The award was created in 1989 to allow the members of the AARC to select and recognize the top providers of respiratory products and services. Association members evaluate nominees on six criteria: quality of equipment, accessibility and helpfulness of sales personnel, responsiveness, service record, truth in advertising and support of the respiratory care profession. In 1996, the Zenith Award was given to just five of the more than 400 companies in the industry.

Similarly, HealthShare/THA gives an award for

Outstanding Service to Texas Hospitals each year at the Texas Hospital Association annual convention. Only endorsed companies are eligible—and they must exhibit an exemplary level of service and caring for the health care industry, industry hospitals and HealthShare/THA.

VarVision gives out Best Vendor and Best Product awards, too. VarVision is a semi-annual meeting of presidents and key executives from the Value Added Reseller (VAR) and Systems Integrator (SI) community, and the award winners are selected solely by votes from these senior industry executives. According to Symantec, winner of the Best Vendor award in 1995 and in 1996, vendors attend the VarVision meetings "to build strong, strategic relationships with these primary decision makers."

In spite of the fact that this award is not familiar to most Americans, it has significant value in its industry—in part because it is not easy to win. "Symantec has achieved the unprecedented by winning the Best Vendor award for the second year in a row," said Peter Eisenhauer, president of VarVision. "This award recognizes that Symantec has successfully demonstrated ongoing commitment to the reseller/integrator channel during the past year with new solutions, technologies and expanded reseller-oriented programs."

"Winning this prestigious award for the second straight year, competing with such seasoned and top-quality vendors, is a real honor for Symantec," said John Bruce, director of worldwide alternate channel sales. "This award recognizes the energy the professionals in our organization have committed to raising the bar over last year's performance by bringing out a host of new and innovative solutions for VARs and Systems Integrators."

Local Awards

While only a few companies will be able to win an award from a large national association, many of these groups also have local chapters. This means even more chances for an association to recognize excellence and further its mission—and even more chances for association members and vendors to win an award, since there are fewer competitors. These awards may mirror the national organization's program, or they may be tailored to a particular area.

For example, the Keystone Chapter of the Associated Builders & Contractors (ABC) presented three awards at the beginning of 1997 at the chapter's annual banquet. The group chose to recognize a Person of the Year and a Specialty Contractor of the Year.

It also gave out a 1996 Legislator of the Year award—to State Senator Gibson E. Armstrong for his efforts to further workers' compensation reform; his bill sponsorship and voting record; and his aid in helping ABC obtain key seats on various state councils and boards. (Talk about using an awards program to further your association's goals!)

Cash Prizes

Associations often use prize money to further their goals, as well. For example, the American Gastroenterological Association has as one of its goals the discovery of a cure for gastric cancer. It awards $50,000 to an investigator to conduct clinical research over a two-year period to develop a cure for the disease.

The American Association for the Advancement of Science awards $5,000 for the Lifetime Mentor Award. And its Newcomb Cleveland Prize is a $5,000 award for outstanding articles published in *Science* magazine.

The academic association known as the Universities Council on Water Resources also gives an annual cash award: a Dissertation/Thesis Award of $500 to the best paper on water conservation.

Whether the award is a trophy, a check or a combination of the two is less important than its role in fulfilling the association's mission. Its function is to demarcate the extraordinary from the ordinary, but an award's legitimacy—derived from its acceptance among the peers who give it and receive it—is its true value.

5 Charity Awards

Charitable donations in the United States for all kinds of causes—from animal welfare to architectural preservation—amounted to $70 billion in 1994 (the latest year for which Internal Revenue Service data were available). According to the IRS, charitable giving ranks only behind state and local taxes as the most frequently claimed deduction, showing up—at an average of about $2,400—on a quarter of all individual tax returns.

There is even a professional society for raising charity monies. The National Society of Fund Raising Executives states as its purpose:

> ... the profound conviction that a vital component of the guarantee of human freedom and social creativity is the preservation of the opportunity for people, freely and voluntarily, to form organizations to meet a perceived need or advocate a cause, and to seek funds in support of these activities.

Whether they are run by volunteers or managed by professionals, charities raise money through celebrity golf tournaments, auctions, car washes, bake sales, galas ... and awards programs.

Many of the larger charities clearly have mastered

the use of the awards ceremony—both as a way to raise a significant sum of money in a single evening and as a way to raise the public's awareness of their cause.

Whether you plan to help your favorite charity—or other association—launch an awards program or you intend to set up one for your business, there is much to be learned by studying the awards ceremonies of successful charities.

The Sports Legends Gala

The Paralysis Project raises money to fund research to find a cure for spinal cord injury paralysis. Every year, the charity stages the Sports Legends gala to honor luminaries from the world of sports.

Why? Because people will buy tickets to attend an event at which they can rub elbows with, get autographs from and have their pictures taken with famous athletes. (For variations on this type of fund-raiser, substitute any other genre of celebrity for "athletes"— e.g., "soap opera stars," "famous writers." The genre of celebrity is important only insofar as it appeals to the target audience of ticket buyers, and it is possible and practical to get the celebs to the event.)

Tickets are sold for an evening of dinner, dancing, a silent auction and the principal event, the presentation of the athletes. Film clips are shown recounting highlights of each athlete's career, then each athlete is presented with a memento of the evening—a loving cup or a plaque. Each of the athletes also has a chance to give a brief acceptance speech. (At this sort of event, if the athletes are properly briefed on the charity and its goals, not only will they give a gracious acceptance speech, but they will speak to the mission of the charity and their support for its work.)

The net profits from the event—which can be substantial—go into the research fund to find a cure for spinal cord injuries.

The Victor Sports Awards, given by the City of Hope National Medical Center, are the most well-known and successful variation on the Sports Legends. The Victor's 30th anniversary in 1996 was marked by an awards show from the Las Vegas Hilton Hotel that was telecast live on Prime Sports Network. It featured an all-star cast of championship athletes and celebrity presenters.

The weekend of fundraising also included a golf tournament, in which generous donors paid to be part of celebrity/athlete foursomes, and a sports memorabilia auction.

According to David Marmel, the executive producer of the Victors, the continuing success of the awards rests on:

1) tradition—because every athlete honored in a particular category can look back on his or her most illustrious peers having received the award in the past, and to receive a Victor is nothing less than to join a pantheon;

2) philanthropy—because everyone involved with the event is aware of the research dollars being raised and contributed to the City of Hope;

3) location—the awards are hosted by the Las Vegas Hilton; and

4) star power—after the winner in each category

The Victor Sports Awards

is known, an entertainment celebrity is solicited to present that winner's award. Prestigious athletes naturally attract prestigious entertainers, which gives the event a double dose of stardom.

Another major sports legends award benefiting charity (the V foundation for cancer research, in this case) is the ESPY, given by the ESPN sports network. Unlike the Victors, which pre-announce the winner in each category, ESPY gives its telecast an air of dramatic anticipation by announcing the winner from a field of nominees in each category. By doing so, ESPY is not so much a "tribute" event as a conventional awards show, à la the Emmys or Oscars.

Much as the Victors exploit their core fundraising event with supplementary "ramping" activities (e.g., their celebrity/paying-guest golf tournament), ESPN promotes its telecast with an earlier-in-the-week fashion show that determines the best-looking uniform in each of the four major team sports. The five nominated jerseys in each category are modeled at a photo-op friendly luncheon event—the press always likes to attend events where food is served—at which sports celebrities and supermodels are in attendance.

In 1997, the Pistons took the honors for the National Basketball Association, the Raiders for the National Football League, the Mighty Ducks for the National Hockey League and the Yankees for major league baseball. The Ducks also won the honors for the most fashionable uniform in all sports.

Charity "cause awards," such as those given by Junior Achievement chapters around the country, are events that follow the "rubbing elbows with celebrities" paradigm of Sports Legends fundraisers.

For example, in an article titled "Honoring an Original Perfect Role Model," the *Los Angeles Times* reported on a Southern California Junior Achievement event at which Gene Autry received the Spirit of Achievement Award in 1996.

According to the *Times*:

> Gene Autry's Cowboy Code lists 10 credos. Among them are No. 1: "The cowboy must never shoot first, hit a smaller man or take unfair advantage." No. 3: "He must always tell the truth." No. 6: "He must help people in distress." No. 7: "He must be a good worker."

The article also called Autry "the perfect role model for youth."

The event, hosted by chairman Michael Eisner of the Walt Disney Co., drew 700 business leaders. The proceeds went to the coffers of the SoCal Junior Achievement chapter.

Another example of a cause award is the Kennedy Center Honors, which raises money in support of the Kennedy Center for the Performing Arts in Washington, D.C. In 1996, the awards went to a number of performing arts legends, including playwright Edward Albee, jazz composer and instrumentalist Benny Carter, country music star Johnny Cash, actor Jack Lemmon and ballerina Maria Tallchief. The televised presentation of awards is the final event in a weekend of fundraising dinners, brunches and receptions attended by an array of political and entertainment celebrities, including President and Mrs. Clinton.

Rewarding Businesses

There are also charity awards that recognize businesses' contributions, in terms of fundraising or furthering a charity's goals. This hybrid of charity and business awards is exemplified by the Spirit of America Awards, sponsored by United Way of America. The awards honor companies and employees for overall excellence in building stronger, healthier communities in partnership with United Way. They simultaneously recognize business leadership while encouraging that same business leadership to continue its support of charitable giving.

United Way also sponsors a companion award, called the Alexis de Tocqueville Society Award, which recognizes the accomplishments and contributions of individuals to their communities.

Similarly, the American Red Cross gives the Philos Award to corporations and the Good Neighbor Award to individuals who best exemplify the spirit of charitable giving.

Numerous charities also hold special events, sometimes known as donor dances or donor luncheons, which require a donation of a certain amount to attend—and can be seen as a way of rewarding people or companies that have given substantial amounts to their causes. A variation on this theme are events held for volunteers who have put in a certain number of hours.

Our hypothetical Widget Co. is a fictional example of a business being rewarded for its involvement with a charity. In that case, at the suggestion of Betty (who won the Good Egg Award for her efforts), the Widget

Co. employees donated the money set aside for their annual Christmas party to Charity X. In turn, Charity X gave the Widget Co. its Angel Award, which honors an individual or company that has made a significant contribution toward the fight to end Disease Y.

Businesses that win awards from charities often get considerable exposure, in terms of press coverage. They also build good will—especially when they are involved in a local charity or a cause that is seen as particularly important in their community.

In his syndicated newspaper column, humorist Art Buchwald has identified a generic type of charity award, known as the Man of the Year Award:

The Generic "Man of the Year Award"

> Once the man of the year is selected and the committee decides that it can get enough people to turn out for the evening, the call is made to the lucky recipient, telling him that the country wishes to pay homage to his civic and charitable work.
>
> The one rub is if the person is not available that night, he can't be man of the year. Everyone knows that you can't have a man of the year dinner without a man. So the committee says that it's sorry, but it will have to find another man of the year—one who will show up.
>
> The man of the year dinners are very touching.
>
> This is because the man being honored is counted on to buy 10 tables for his family. The other tables are sold to people who do business with him and are afraid not to buy in case they lose the account.

... Once everything is in place ... the honoree's golfing partner, his tax attorney and grandson speak glowingly about him, while at the other end of the ballroom the chairman is counting the take.

While Buchwald has a knack for putting a cynical spin on such endeavors, there certainly are myriad Man of the Year charitable awards—and they have been known to net quite a lot of money for the charity. Steven Spielberg was honored at such a gala in January 1997. The *Los Angeles Times* reported that he had been "sought after by the American Jewish Committee for years" to accept its Sherrill C. Corwin Human Relations Award, to no avail.

But, because Mr. Spielberg "truly exemplifies the family values and Jewish values and the human spirit" honored by this award, his friend and attorney (who also chairs the American Jewish Committee) finally "prevailed" on him to accept the award. In accepting it at a gala dinner at the Regent Beverly Wilshire Hotel's grand ballroom, Mr. Spielberg pledged his continued support of humanitarian efforts. As proof, he announced a gift of $500,000 to the organization that honored him with its award.

Do the Right Thing

Supporting charities and causes is an opportunity for everyone within a company to work together selflessly for the benefit of others and/or the community. It is "the right thing to do," socially responsible and very likely "politically correct." But it is also a way to encourage teamwork, motivate employees, build morale, create awareness, increase loyalty, and enhance the employees' and the company's image in the community and among customers.

If there was ever a win-win proposition, it is a company's support of charities. And there is no better way to raise funds for a good cause than through carefully designed and implemented awards programs.

6   Entering Awards Competitions

"Businesswomen Are in Good Hands With Allstate and Avon," proclaimed the headline in the *Los Angeles Times*. Why? Because it had just been announced that both Avon and Allstate would be receiving the prestigious Catalyst Award in March 1997, an annual prize given by the nonprofit Catalyst Group as part of its efforts to help women rise in business.

Needless to say, in an era in which sexual harassment and discrimination lawsuits are constantly making headlines, this kind of press is a great way to woo talented women—and other people in search of a good work environment—to your business.

"To win the Catalyst Award is to lead the nation in taking advantage of the rich talent now available," Paul Allaire, chairman and chief executive of Xerox Corp. and a member of the New York-based Catalyst Group's board of directors, told the *Times*.

What does it take to win?

Catalyst considers senior management's commitment to women's advancement, the originality of a company's efforts and the measurable results shown by those efforts. For example, Allstate Insurance Co. gives merit raises to managers who hire and retain women and minorities. Overall, Catalyst praised the insurer's in-depth efforts to create and then reach its diversity goals.

"We have women who are well-positioned throughout Allstate," said Jennise Henry, director of diversity and affirmative action at Allstate. "But it's not something you can do overnight. It's a process that Allstate has been working on since the 1960s."

Having a plan and following it in a serious and creative way has been paying off. According to Catalyst, the 500 largest U.S. companies have a total of 12,885 corporate officers—about 10 percent of whom are women. In contrast, as of December 1996, 19 percent of the corporate officers at Allstate were women (up from 16 percent six years prior).

Avon was honored with a Catalyst Award for its efforts in Mexico, a country better known for *machismo* than for promoting female executives. And yet Avon Mexico has been able to use its annual review to identify employees with high potential—and to track women's progress in the company. The payoff: 31 percent of the top managers in Avon Mexico were women in 1996, compared with 24 percent in 1993.

According to the *Times*, "Avon Mexico supports breast cancer research, women's athletics and cultural activities in Mexico to encourage women's advances outside the company."

"Avon Mexico has approached women's progress from every aspect of the business," added Marcia Worthing, senior vice president of human resources at New York-based Avon.

The Catalyst Award has done much to enhance the image of Avon and Allstate. And publicizing the award's criteria and the recipients' winning techniques is sure to help other businesses attract and promote women and minorities—which might be called the "trickle-down effect" of any successful awards program.

Winning
Awards Boosts
Morale

When a company wins an award, it clearly is good for business in a number of ways—and building morale is not least among them. Take Pioneer Industries as an example.

The Seattle-based manufacturing firm produces sheetmetal parts for such customers as Boeing, Heart Interface and Quinton Instruments. It also specializes in hiring an unusual work force.

Most of the company's employees have never successfully held a job before. Many are on work release from prison. And about 75 percent of Pioneer's work force either has been or is currently in a drug or alcohol recovery program, David Guth, executive vice president of Pioneer Industries, told the *Seattle Post-Intelligencer*. Before coming to Pioneer, many of these employees lacked even the basic social skills required to function in the workplace.

Perhaps even more remarkable still, the company invites turnover. That's because its goals extend beyond producing sheetmetal parts. The self-supporting business also produces marketable, productive employees.

Part of the goal of working at Pioneer is to become skilled enough to be employable on the "outside," said Guth. About 25 people "graduate" from the company's basic training program each quarter, and many of them do go into the local work force.

"In a training environment, by definition you're building in turnover," said Gary Mulhair, president of Pioneer Human Services, the parent organization that oversees Pioneer Industries, as well as a group of work-release programs, chemical dependency and mental health treatment facilities, alcohol- and drug-free housing units, and various other sheltered workshop facilities.

Since this is a book about awards, you may have guessed what's coming next. Pioneer won an award for its humanitarian efforts, right?

Actually, in December 1996, the company became the first nonprofit, sheltered workshop in Washington state to receive an international quality certification: the ISO 9002 designation. (While ISO certification is not an award, per se, we do discuss the merits of gaining certification on page 91.) In fact, only 75 other companies in the entire state have been awarded this designation, after having met stringent requirements for work quality and customer service.

To maintain these sorts of quality standards in this sort of work environment is a remarkable accomplishment.

Pioneer, clearly, is a remarkable company—and an internal awards program is one of the keys to the company's success. The facility's walls are lined with bulletin boards that hold pictures of employees being recognized for their efforts. According to the *Seattle Post-Intelligencer*, "Some cradle their awards or certificates as though they'd never held anything like it before."

The company recognizes employees' efforts—and their often-difficult financial circumstances. Because so many of the workers have children and are struggling financially, Guth said, the company conducts fundraisers year-round to make sure every child of a company worker gets a gift during the holidays.

Pioneer's remarkable efforts paid off with the ISO certification. But they also are felt on the bottom line (a figure most nonprofits would prefer not to discuss). Contributing to the business's financial health is a reduction in workers' comp claims. The company, which is self-insured, listens to workers on safety issues—and this has led to an accident rate that is one-sixth what it was when the firm insured through the state.

Pioneer's efforts are saving taxpayers money, too. According to the *Post-Intelligencer*, "Of the 150 women who have come to the company from correctional facilities since 1991, only 11 have gone back to prison, a recidivism rate less than half the overall rate for women."

Throwing Your Hat Into the Ring

Business awards clearly can do great things for a company and its employees. But, most of the time, your company can't win if you don't enter the competition.

Even as you continually gather information about markets, clients, means of increasing efficiency, government regulations and other business essentials, you should keep current on awards possibilities. Here are four sources of information:

- If you are a member of an association, you probably already receive a journal or newsletter that carries information about relevant awards programs. (It is a safe assumption that there are any number of relevant awards programs, so if your association does not advertise them, notify the executive director that you want more membership service in the area of awards notifications.)

- Some industries have their own competition alerts that you can subscribe to. For example, Nova Communications publishes a monthly newsletter (*Ad & PR Awards Competition Alert*) for the advertising and public relations industry. Readers are advised of deadlines, entry procedures, eligibility and all other pertinent information—including tips on what the judges look for in a successful entry.

- The Internet is an excellent source of information about relevant awards competitions. For example, if you search the Worldwide Web for "pharmaceutical awards," you find useful awards information for Research Triangle Institute's Pharmaceutical Pioneers Awards, the American Association of Pharmaceutical Scientists' Awards, the American Society of Health-System Pharmacists Awards and the Pharmacology-Morphology Association Fellowship Awards, among many others.

If you are an arborist, the Internet will notify you of the National Arborist Association Excellence in Arboriculture Awards Competition. Or if your business is tire manufacturing, look to the Net for information about the Louisiana Transportation Research Center's Transportation Innovation for Research Exploration (TIRE) Awards.

- Gale Research's *Awards, Honors and Prizes* is the definitive awards reference book. The 13th edition (1997) of Volume 1 (United States and Canada) lists approximately 17,000 awards bestowed by some 5,000 organizations. Its subject index is especially useful. For example, if you are looking for competitions in the dairy industry, there is a listing of 30 such awards. Hair stylists have six awards listed; educational film makers, four; accountants and sanitary engineers, 44 each; and rodeo clowns and riders, a total of nine.

Take It From the Top

The premier business award in the United States is the Malcolm Baldrige National Quality Award, which recognizes and promotes business excellence and quality achievement. It was established in 1987 and named for a distinguished secretary of commerce who served under President Reagan.

The prestige associated with this award is exemplified by the presentation location: no less a site than the White House.

What makes this particular award so important? At the 1996 awards presentation, President Clinton said:

Quality is one of the keys to the continued competitive success of U.S. businesses. The Malcolm Baldrige National Quality Award, which highlights customer satisfaction, work force empowerment and increased productivity, has come to symbolize America's commitment to excellence.

There are three eligibility categories for Baldrige Awards. Awards may be given in each category each year, and are based on a review of applications submitted by:

- manufacturing companies;
- service companies; and
- small businesses.

Unlike the kind of business-to-business awards we discussed in Chapter 3—and touch on again later in this chapter—the Baldridge is a public/private partnership award, with a complex administrative structure comprised of six separate tiers:

- The Foundation for the Malcolm Baldrige National Quality Award, which raises funds to permanently endow the costs of administering the award program;

- The United States Department of Commerce, which has overall responsibility for the award;

- The National Institute of Scientific Testing (NIST), an agency of the Commerce Department's Technology Administration, which manages the award program;

- The American Society for Quality Control (ASQC), which administers the award program under contract to NIST;

- The Board of Overseers, a committee of distinguished leaders from all sectors of the U.S. economy that is appointed by the Secretary of Commerce, and which is charged with recommending changes and improvements in the awards program; and

- The Board of Examiners, a group of business and quality experts who evaluate the award applications and make recommendations to NIST.

While the Baldrige Awards process is rigorous, it offers numerous benefits for every company that decides to compete. That's because the Baldrige Awards are designed to increase the business efficiency and productivity of all competitors—"to serve as a working tool for managing performance, planning, training and assessment."

Within the applying company, the awards are designed to promote:

- awareness of quality as an increasingly important element in competitiveness;

- understanding of the requirements for performance excellence; and

- sharing of information on successful performance strategies and the benefits derived from implementation of these strategies.

These, in turn, are meant to "help companies enhance their competitiveness through focus on dual, results-oriented goals." Those goals are:

The Benefits of Competition

- delivery of ever-improving value to customers, resulting in marketplace success; and

- improvement of overall company performance and capabilities.

"Utilizing the Malcolm Baldrige Award criteria can help you focus on improvement areas," writes an executive experienced with the application and review procedures. "Applying for the award is a good way to receive some outside evaluation of your process and benchmark yourself against others. The criteria of the awards help you to project key requirements for delivering ever-improving value to customers, while at the same time maximizing the overall effectiveness and productivity of the organization."

In 1988, Merix Corp. of Forest Grove, Oregon, began using the criteria for the Malcolm Baldrige National Quality Award as a self-assessment tool. The company also decided to apply for the award so that it would receive valuable third-party feedback from the examination team.

The company didn't proceed far enough in the competition to actually merit an on-site review until 1994. But, in the interim, it learned several things from applying the award criteria. According to *National Productivity Review*:

> [The] planning cycle yielded an improved process for establishing goals and operational plans that are aligned throughout the company. This all-encompassing continuous improvement culture keeps Merix in a leadership position in the interconnect industry and results in exemplary financial performance.

When Merix finally received a site evaluation in 1994, it was an exciting affirmation of the firm's self-assessment and improvement strategies. Although the company didn't bring home an award that year, it did receive a 40-page feedback report from the award examiners based on their detailed on-site assessment of the entire organization.

Merix also decided to incorporate the Shingo Prize criteria into its self-assessment program, and eventually applied for that prize as well. It is named for—and based on the philosophy of—Shigeo Shingo, the man responsible for Toyota's just-in-time production system. Shingo was driven to eliminate waste in its many forms, which include overproduction, queue time, transportation time, process time, excess inventory, excess motion and defects.

The Shingo Prize criteria examine the applicant's:

- organizational focus on higher value-added issues;

- business processes as arenas for analysis and improvement;

- acceptance and use of Shingo's view of waste as any non-value-added activity;

- effectiveness of tools and techniques in improvement activities; and

- cooperation and integration at all levels.

A company must fill out an Achievement Report to apply. The examiners evaluate the results described in this report using the following criteria:

- improvement trend in each key area;

- performance level and use of outside benchmarks in intelligent goal setting;

- selection, adjustment and use of appropriate measures; and

- intelligent use of measured results to stimulate further improvement.

Total Quality

The prototype of business awards that recognize and promote business excellence and quality achievement is the Deming Prize. Named after Total Quality Management (TQM) guru W. Edwards Deming, the award was established by the Japan Union of Scientists and Engineers (JUSE) in 1951. At that time, JUSE had become keenly interested in Deming's philosophy of quality control as a means of resurrecting Japan from its post-World War II ruin.

"The nation's industrial base was in ruins. The once prosperous populace had gone without consumer goods, then without food for the wartime effort. Their cities had also been destroyed," Dr. Mohsen Attaran and Heather D. Fitzgerald wrote in *Industrial Management*. "But postwar Japan, a nation poor in material resources but rich in people, embraced the advice, knowledge and expertise of Deming, contributing to the beginnings of a global economic superpower."

According to Ricoh, Deming's TQM philosophy includes the customer as the ultimate definer of the quality of a firm's products or services. Feedback from the customer becomes the criteria for the design or redesign of all aspects of production, with the goal being to meet or exceed "customers' changing expectations for product performance."

This is achieved by constant attention to the 14 points of "management by positive cooperation" that Deming said would create a "new climate" of organizational culture consisting of "joy in work, innovation and cooperation":

1) Create constancy of purpose for improvement of product and service.

2) Adopt the new philosophy: Mistakes and negativism are unacceptable.

3) Cease dependence on mass inspection. Require instead statistical evidence that quality is built in to eliminate the need for inspection on a mass basis.

4) End the practice of awarding business on the basis of price tag alone. Instead, depend on meaningful measures of quality along with price.

5) Improve constantly and forever the system of production and service.

6) Institute a vigorous training program of education and retraining.

7) Institute leadership.

8) Drive out fear so that everyone may work effectively for the company.

9) Break down barriers between departments.

10) Eliminate numerical goals, posters and slogans for the work force that ask for new levels of productivity without providing new methods.

11) Eliminate work standards that prescribe numerical quotas.

12) Remove barriers to pride of workmanship.

13) Encourage education and self-improvement for everyone.

14) Take action to accomplish the transformation.

In addition to being a prescription for management by positive cooperation, these 14 points are the core criteria for the Deming Prize, which is awarded annually by the JUSE to one or more companies that have demonstrated sustained TQM in the areas of corporate policy, quality systems, education and training, results and future plans.

As the Fuji Photo Optical Co. noted after winning a 1996 Deming Prize for what the jury called "continuous activities since 1991 for the outstanding improvement of our corporate management through quality control," the prize is "the most prestigious honor among corporations for quality control systems in Japan."

Remarks from other participants listed in *The Deming Prize Guide for Overseas Companies* (1996 edition) reflect the same positive response to the competition—and underscore the benefits of entering:

- "The examination was very helpful because the examiners pointed out issues we had not recognized before."

- "By establishing specific targets and a date for the Deming Prize examination, our

TQM progressed much faster and was better disseminated to the rank and file."

- "The things we thought we could not achieve in the past—or the things that might have taken five, 10 years practicing business as usual—have been speeded up and achieved."

- "During the process leading up to the Deming Prize examination, the company as a whole focused on improving product and service quality, and the organizational constitution was strengthened. These efforts have contributed to breaking down sectionalism, improving interdepartmental communications, removing barriers between departments and instilling a sense of unity."

- "We have become much better at interdepartmental communications and cross-functional management."

The Deming Prize is also a coveted business award in the United States, where Florida Power and Light and AT&T Power Systems have both won. After AT&T won in 1994, a spokesman said, "People want to be empowered and involved. Together, we combined the discipline of TQM with the creativity of the individuals in our work force. We adapted Japanese TQM to American manufacturing culture by building on the individuality of American workers."

Even if your company is not yet prepared to enter this sort of awards competition, you certainly can benefit from studying the awards criteria and applying these ideas to your business.

State-Based Awards

State-based awards, such as the Rhode Island Quality Awards Programs, are a local variation on the national Baldrige awards. As such, they have the advantage of being more customized and specific to local companies and their business culture—while still offering the same opportunities for quality improvement that make the Baldriges so valuable.

The Rhode Island program has categories for:

- agriculture, forestry, fisheries, mining;

- construction;

- manufacturing;

- transportation, communications, public utilities;

- wholesale and retail trade;

- service organization—finance, insurance, real estate, business services, professional services; and

- other (specify).

The awards program is administered by the Rhode Island Area Coalition for Excellence (RACE), which is comprised of members from business, government, education, professional organizations and the general public. These awards promote both business (à la the Baldrige criteria and general procedures) and education.

Mississippi has a similar awards program, which is part of the annual Excellence in Mississippi conference. The conference is held each year so businesses can share ways of improving quality. In 1996, workshops covered proactively managing conflict in the workplace, building high-performance organizations and teams, and communicating effectively. During a luncheon at the close of the conference, Gov. Kirk Fordice presented the State Board for Community and Junior Colleges' Mississippi Quality Awards to 41 businesses. These awards were divided into four levels: Quality Interest, Quality Commitment, the Excellence Award and the Governor's Award.

In 1995, Baxter Healthcare took home the top honor: the Governor's Award. In '96, the company's employees were back to present a workshop called "Been There, Done That, and Looking for More," about how the company's involvement of all employees in management for quality and productivity is producing product value for customers.

The awards program relies on volunteer examiners from businesses in the state. According to the *Mississippi Business Journal*, a board of 111 examiners helped the judges make their decisions by reviewing the applications and visiting every site. Jeniece Crum, quality engineer for Dover Elevator Systems in Walnut, was one of the examiners in 1996. She signed up to be an examiner because she wanted to learn more about the criteria, in case Dover Elevator Systems decided to enter the competition in the future.

ISO Certification

Although ISO 9000 certification is not an award per se, it functions like an award. Set up by the International Standards Organization (ISO) in 1987, the "9000" is a set of global standards for both quality management and quality assurance that has been adopted by more than 90 countries worldwide. Developed for contractual business relationships when a supplier and its customer are based in different countries, ISO 9000 standards are meant to increase customer confidence in the quality system used by their suppliers by:

- establishing consistent language and terminology;

- providing baseline quality practices that are accepted internationally; and

- reducing the need for costly on-site supplier assessments.

Certification for ISO 9000 status is increasingly desirable among companies that wish to distinguish themselves from their uncertified competitors as they seek international customers. Registered U.S. companies include AT&T, Eastman Kodak, Exxon, GE, IBM, Westinghouse and Xerox.

According to a Dun & Bradstreet analysis, ISO 9000 is important to business because:

- it provides a common set of globally accepted quality standards;

- it is recognized in the European Community as the leading quality management standard;

- manufacturers and service companies both in the U.S. and abroad use ISO 9000 certification to benchmark their choice of suppliers.

Interleaf, an electronic document service that assists companies in gaining ISO 9000 certification, notes the following about the differences between "9000," the Deming Prize and the Baldrige Awards:

Is "winning" an ISO 9000 certification different from winning a Deming or Baldrige award?

In a broad sense, they each focus on quality. Not just quality of product or service, but rather quality in the process. But there are also important differences.

The Baldrige Award ... represents a finite point, an award that marks an achievement in a given year. There are only a very small number of winners and many "non-winners."

The Deming Prize has no firm requirements other than to meet or exceed customers' needs based on Deming's 14 points, which are often as intangible as "drive out fear."

ISO 9000 is not a one-time award. It opens the door to continuous and ongoing improvement. Under the current ISO 9000 guidelines, organizations must be audited every three years and go through the entire certification process upon expiration of certification.

Finally, every company that achieves ISO 9000 is a "winner." Unregistered companies are the only "losers"—of customers and new business. In the final analysis, ISO 9000 standards will have a much greater impact on business than any quality award.

As with the Deming and Baldrige awards, ISO 9000 certification begins with a company's application, followed by a rigorous assessment of the company's quality by an accredited "registrar" that can take anywhere from six months to two years. Among the check points are:

- **Management responsibility**: Requires procedures to be put in place to define, document and communicate quality policy.

- **Contract review**: Review contracts to assure requirements are adequately defined and assure capability exists to meet requirements.

- **Process control**: Ensure production processes are carried out under controlled conditions.

- **Non-conforming product**: Avoid inadvertent use of non-conforming product.

- **Servicing**: Perform service as required by customer contract.

The benefits to a certified company, as with the Deming and Baldrige awards, are primarily internal increases in productivity and efficiency. But unlike the awards, ISO 9000 also provides specific legal, contractual, cost savings and other benefits. As Interleaf points out:

- **Legal**: In some industries, registration is a legal or mandated requirement to market in the European Community.

- **Cost savings**: ISO 9000 eliminates the need for customer-driven audits.

- **Customer satisfaction**: Customers have more confidence in companies that are ISO 9000 certified.

- **Internal improvement**: ISO 9000 standards are the foundation of higher quality systems that result in improved processes and procedures. "Manufacturing experts agree that ISO 9000 certification provides a solid foundation for developing a TQM system. Many companies implement ISO 9000 programs as a foundation for TQM programs or in pursuit of the Malcolm Baldrige Award."

Furthering standardization is also the mission of the American National Standards Institute (ANSI). According to the Institute, it is a "private non-profit organization [since 1918] that coordinates the U.S. voluntary standards system, bringing together interests from the private and public sectors to develop voluntary standards for a wide array of U.S. industries [for the purpose of enhancing the global competitiveness of U.S. business]. ANSI is the official U.S. member body to the world's leading standards bodies," including the International Standards Organization (the "ISO" of the ISO 9000 certification program).

The Institute's membership includes approximately 1,300 national and international companies, 30 government agencies, 20 institutions and 250 professional, technical, trade, labor and consumer organizations.

ANSI awards are given for:

- promotion of trade and understanding among nations through personal participation in the advancement, development or administration of international standardization, measurement or certification (the Astin-Polk Medal);

- leadership in the actual development and

application of voluntary standards (the Finegan Standards Medal);

- support of standardization as a management tool (the Howard Coonley Medal);

- leadership in the direction and long-range planning of the ANSI standards federation (the George S. Wham Leadership Medal); and

- development of information technology standards (the Edward Lohse Information Technology Medal).

Community Awards Programs

A number of local communities offer awards, too, many of which are administered by the area's Chamber of Commerce.

Local awards, like association awards, offer peer recognition. They also can boost your company's image—and sales—in the community. For a firm that does most of its business locally, these awards can be invaluable.

An example is the annual Business Beautification Award, cosponsored by the Women's Division of the Hampton Roads Chamber of Commerce in Chesapeake, Virginia, and the Chesapeake Environmental Improvement Council. The purpose of the award is to recognize a local business that shows pride in the visual impression it leaves on the surrounding neighborhood, and that displays environmental awareness. Businesses are judged on the quality and maintenance of their building, landscaping, litter control and signs.

The Grand Island Area (Nebraska) Chamber of Commerce gives out a Small Business of the Year

Award. The 1996 winner, Rinder Printing Co., "qualified for this honor based upon its history of corporate citizenship, diversification, sales and payroll growth and its ability to overcome adversity," said Claudia Fredricks, chairwoman of the Small Business Council of the Grand Island Area Chamber of Commerce.

With only 17 employees, Rinder definitely is a small business—and a close-knit one. "Our staff is living testament that we win the wars. We may not win every battle," said Tim White, the company's president. But, he added, "Rinder Printing has been here for 46 years, serving customers and the community."

The company has contributed tens of thousands of dollars in cash and in-kind services to a wide variety of community organizations, White said at the award presentation. "From the Heartland United Way to walk-a-thons, Rinder Printing employees are involved in making Grand Island and Central Nebraska a better place to live."

Making the area a better place to live is the purpose of the Chesapeake Bay Commission, which is dedicated to reducing nutrient pollution in the bay. The commission also gives awards to local businesses. In 1996, Wenger's Feed Mill of Lancaster, Pennsylvania, received the recognition for a feed additive that reduces phosphorus pollution.

Revitalizing the community of Bel Air, Maryland, is the purpose of the Economic and Community Development Commission—a group responsible for soliciting nominations for the Business of the Year and making recommendations to the Town Commissioners.

Bel Air started a Business of the Year award program in 1995 to recognize the important part business plays in the town. Criteria include the contribution of time and effort to town activities by the business, financial contributions in support of town projects, contributions to the economy and culture of the town, and the cooperative nature of the business.

The winner in 1996 was Georgetown North, a restaurant owned by Gary Clark. The restaurant was selected in part because of Clark's work on the Christmas parade for the past seven years, and his role in making the summer lunch concerts "a successful program for the town."

Many communities also have local awards programs honoring women in business and minority-owned businesses. For instance, the town of Jacksonville, Florida, gives a Minority Entrepreneur of the Year Award as part of its Minority Enterprise Development Week. The award criteria include the company's growth over the past year, job creation, financial health and commitment to community involvement.

University Awards Programs

Colleges and universities are also principal sources of business awards. To find out more about these competitions, you may want to contact your alma mater or get in touch with one or more local universities.

For instance, Dickinson College in Carlisle, Pennsylvania, offers:

- the Benjamin Rush Award—to honor the contributions of a member of the business community whose career has exemplified the effectiveness of a liberal arts education in business; and

- the Dickinson College Arts Award—to recognize outstanding business contributions to the creative or performing arts.

Roger Williams University in Providence, Rhode Island, gives an Alumnus of the Year award at its annual alumni weekend. The 1996 recipient, architect Raymond N. Menard '57, said he never saw it coming: "I have never been active in the alumni association. About a year and a half ago, they requested my resume; then I got a call saying my name was being considered for this award. When I won, I was obviously quite honored. I was also surprised."

The university honored Menard "as a graduate who has received significant, long-term success in personal and professional achievements and who has made outstanding contributions to his profession and to the community."

A major recipient of the University of Georgia's George Foster Peabody Awards is the Home Box Office cable network (HBO), whose programming has won 14 Peabodys since 1981. The mission of the Peabodys is the recognition of distinguished achievement and the most meritorious public service rendered by electronically delivered programming (radio, television and cable).

In an unusual case of awarding the awards givers, HBO announced in late 1996 that it was giving the university $10,000 a year for three years to create a fund so independent producers would be able to enter the Peabody competition. The contribution is "to defray the cost of entering the competition for independent filmmakers, investigative reporters, international producers and others who might otherwise find the entry fee prohibitive."

HBO's contribution was meant to further the mission of the Peabodys by encouraging the production of innovative electronic journalism.

(Because HBO—a Time Warner division—is a far cry from the struggling world of independent producers short on entry money, its contribution could not be construed as a conflict of interest.)

Business-to-Business Awards

We discussed the benefits of creating a program to award other businesses in Chapter 3—and the rewards of such an awards program clearly go both ways.

For instance, when IEC Electronics Corp. hit a safety milestone—more than 1,200 employees at the company's Newark facility worked more than 1 million hours without a lost-time accident—it was honored with an award by its insurance company, ITT Hartford. Clearly, everyone benefits in this sort of situation: Employees have a safe place to work, the company experiences gains in productivity, the insurer doesn't have to pay a lot of claims—and the company can expect reduced (or at least stable) insurance rates. To reward its employees for their safety efforts, IEC also held an Employee Appreciation Day, during which ITT Hartford presented the firm with its award for One Million Hours.

Union Pacific Railroad also presents a safety award, the Chemical Transportation Safety Pinnacle Award, to companies that have done an outstanding job in performing safe loading techniques and preventing non-accidental chemical releases. (A non-accidental chemical release is an unintentional release of a hazardous material while in transportation that does not usually involve an accident, for example a release caused by a leaking valve.)

Nineteen companies won the Pinnacle Award at the start of 1997, which was based on shipping experience in 1995. Among the five companies that shipped more than 3,000 cars and won was Eastman Chemical Co.

"The award criteria were for a shipper to have zero non-accidental releases on the Union Pacific system and to practice safe loading techniques," said David DeVault of Eastman's Logistics Division. "This Pinnacle Award presented today recognizes the hard work by Eastman employees nationwide to prevent non-accidental releases and ensure we're fulfilling our commitment to protect the public."

Eastman has won similar awards from Conrail, which recognized the company with its Conrail Diamond Drop Award for Flawless Shipping in 1993, 1994 and 1995.

Auto Alliance, a joint venture between Mazda Motor Corp. and Ford Motor Co., awards outstanding vendors with the Auto Alliance Quality Award for Total Excellence. In 1996, the company selected 39 suppliers out of 198 to receive the award. Award criteria are maintaining low returns for the year, product performance and industry-best responsiveness.

Magazine Awards

We also referred in Chapter 3 to numerous magazine awards—and to the tremendous marketing opportunities they create for the award recipients. While many of these awards programs do not require you to formally enter the competition, you can't win if the magazine has never heard of you or your product.

This is where your public relations department (or consultant) comes in. Identify the magazine awards that you believe your company or its products are qualified for. Then let the magazine know about them by sending out letters and/or press releases. (Many magazine editors are working on tight deadlines and may not have the time to spend discussing your company on the phone.)

For instance, each September, *Working Mother* magazine publishes the Working Mother 100, a list of America's most innovative and advanced companies that support a balance between work and family life. The criteria used in assembling the list are compensation, opportunities for women to advance, support for child care, flexibility (flextime, job sharing, part-time) and family-friendly benefits (such as job-protected leave for childbirth, adoption aid, elder care service and referrals).

In 1996, Eli Lilly and Co. was ranked among the Top 10—and the magazine named its CEO, Randy Tobias, Family Champion of the Year.

"I'm very proud—personally and on behalf of all employees at Eli Lilly and Co.—to be among so many recognized champions of work and family issues," Tobias said. "At Lilly, our goal is to help working families have both a good living and a good life. I hope and intend to see initiatives that improve work and family life continue, both at Lilly and in our communities."

Tobias added: "We see bottom-line value in helping employees balance their commitment to Lilly and their commitment to their families. That's good business.

"You can't hire part of a person. You get the sore back along with the skillful hands. You get the anxious heart along with the educated brain. Corporations will succeed and work and family programs will be effective only if they bow to this reality and address employees as whole human beings. Every element of our strategy boils down to people; it acknowledges that our most important resources walk out of our facilities every day and head for home."

However, even with its enlightened leadership, Eli Lilly might never have made it onto *Working Mother's* list if someone hadn't written in requesting an application and more information a few years back. Since then, the magazine has sent the company an application automatically each year.

Since 1990, *Industry Week* has conducted an annual search for plants that exemplify excellence in manufacturing. Nomination forms are published in the magazine. Plants that are nominated receive detailed, 19-page questionnaires, which they submit, along with a supporting statement elaborating on their achievements. Topics covered in the questionnaire include performance, quality, customer focus, technology, community involvement, environmental and safety programs, and competitiveness.

In 1996, 170 facilities were nominated. A panel of judges reviewed the completed entries and narrowed the field to 25 finalists. The finalists then received a second questionnaire, which the judges read before completing the evaluation with a site visit.

Making it into the Top 10 in 1996 was a Dana Corp. Driveshaft Division plant in Bristol, Virginia. Plant personnel attributed the selection to the strides the company has made in achieving a lean staff, flat organizational structure and an emphasis on employee involvement and team work. Between 1991 and 1995, cycle times for the plant's major product were down 55 percent.

To improve its business, the Dana Corp. has been using a Quality Leadership Awards program, based on the Baldrige Award measurements, to evaluate and improve the performance of Dana Divisions in key categories since 1992.

"We're teaching people throughout Dana to measure their products and performance continuously," said Dana Chairman and CEO Southwood J. Morcott. "The recognition that Bristol and other Dana operations are receiving shows that our quality processes are working."

In addition to the *Industry Week* honors, Dana's leasing operation, Dana Commercial Credit, received the Malcolm Baldrige National Quality Award in the service category in 1996.

Quality is essential to Dana's style of management, according to Bob Fesenmyer, general manager of the Driveshaft Division. "We believe Dana people should accept only total quality in everything they do," he said. "And we believe in continuous improvement to ensure our products and processes are the best. The Dana Quality Leadership Award criteria give us objective measures for achieving those goals."

As a winner in the *Industry Week* competition, the Bristol plant was featured on the magazine's *Manage-*

ment Today television program on CNBC. The plant also will be invited to send representatives to the magazine's America's Best Plants conferences in 1997.

Other Sources of Awards

Trusts and foundations also give business awards. For example, the Business Enterprise Trust's Business Enterprise Awards are given to business people and organizations that demonstrate socially concerned business leadership. The awards reflect the trust's philosophy that corporations which serve their constituencies in creative and morally thoughtful ways also serve their shareholders best.

The Freedoms Foundation at Valley Forge follows suit with an extensive program of national awards that "honor and publicly recognize corporations, individuals, organizations and schools who promote, through words and deeds, an understanding of responsible citizenship and the benefits of a free society."

In addition to awards recognizing standardization goals, business excellence and educational efforts, there are also numerous awards given to companies and individuals for public service. For instance, the Jefferson Award for Outstanding Public Service Benefitting Communities is given annually by the American Institute for Public Service in Washington, D.C. The business award was established in part by then-First Lady Jacqueline Kennedy, and the presentation is made at the U.S. Supreme Court.

Even more famous are the Nobel Prizes, awarded annually by the Nobel Foundation—in physiology or medicine, chemistry and physics, literature, economics and for the promulgation of world peace.

Each year, the respective committees send individual invitations to thousands of scientists, members of academies and university professors in numerous countries, asking them to nominate candidates for the Nobel Prizes for the coming year. Those who are competent to submit nominations are chosen in such a way that as many countries and universities as possible will be represented.

The nominations received by each committee are then investigated with the help of specially appointed experts. When the committees have made their selection among the nominated candidates and have presented their recommendations to the prize-awarding institutions, a vote is taken for the final choice of laureates.

The prizes are awarded at a ceremony at the Concert Hall in Stockholm, Sweden, on December 10 (the anniversary of Alfred Nobel's death). The Nobel Peace Prize is awarded on the same day at the City Hall in Oslo, Norway.

Nomination of candidates is restricted. For example, nominations for the physics and chemistry category may come only from a limited group of individuals:

- Swedish and foreign members of the Academy of Sciences;

- Members of the Nobel Committees for Physics and Chemistry;

- Scientists who have been awarded the Prize by the Academy of Sciences;

- Permanent and assistant professors in the

sciences of physics and chemistry at the universities and institutes of technology of Sweden, Denmark, Finland, Iceland and Norway, and the Karolinska Institute;

- Holders of corresponding chairs in at least six universities or university colleges selected by the Academy of Sciences with a view to ensuring the appropriate distribution over the different countries and their seats of learning;

- Other scientists from whom the Academy may see fit to invite proposals.

While the Nobel Prize is awarded to an individual, not a company, it often has been given for a product developed under a firm's aegis. For instance, Kary B. Mullis won the 1993 Nobel Laureate in Chemistry for his invention of the polymerase chain reaction (PCR) method. (Polymerase chain reaction is a technique that amplifies DNA, enabling scientists to make millions— or even billions—of copies of a DNA molecule in a very short time.)

Mullis clearly invented PCR on his own—while cruising on his motorcycle down the Pacific Coast Highway, to be precise—but the idea became the property of his employer at the time, Cetus Corp. of Emeryville, California, which paid him $10,000 for the rights to what has been hailed as the most important discovery in molecular biology in decades.

The Nobels are a famous and historical part of the overall award mix, but their restricted access is the exception that proves the rule:

Reach Out and
Win

Most awards worth having are within the reach of companies that pursue them.

In an attempt to anticipate and address the reluctance of companies to commit the resources of time, personnel and money to an awards preparation that "is indeed hard," the Deming rules book notes the following "misunderstandings" that many businesses have as they wonder if it is worth it to enter the competition:

1) **A small company cannot win**. The size of the company is irrelevant. "When applicant companies practice TQM suited to their business and scope and achieve distinctive results, they will be qualified prize recipients."

2) **Winning the prize is the principal and final goal of competing for it**. "The Deming Prize is a means to promote TQM, not a goal in and of itself. Companies that want a famous award in their trophy cabinet may get it, but they won't necessarily achieve long-term, satisfactory TQM results."

3) **Competing for the prize is too costly and disruptive of day-to-day work**. When expenditures are examined, "they often include expenses for education, standardization and overtime work and on new spending for functions that the company should have made anyway, such as factory equipment, reliability testing, testing equipment or even building a new conference room. In most

cases, these expenses and the extra energy required for the Deming Prize examination were incurred because the companies finally made the decision to do things they had always wanted to do and took advantage of the Deming Prize challenge to do them. These expenses are necessary costs for introducing and promoting TQM, whether a company applies for the examination or not. When these expenses are properly spent, they are of the type of expenses that will pay off in a short period of time and will soon produce higher profits.

"Furthermore, the notion of 'disturbing day-to-day work' is derived from the same root as the misunderstanding that says TQM and day-to-day work are two separate items. In any company, day-to-day work should include managing the quality of products and services, as well as the quality of work performed. Companies that have not previously been doing this will find that, temporarily, they will be busier. This situation arises when they find themselves doing things they should have been doing all along. In the long run, the effects derived from implementing systems for cooperation or improved human relations, for example, are much greater than the efforts required to establish them."

In conclusion, the Deming rules book spells out what should be the goal of all companies that are thinking about entering into awards competitions:

that the organizational constitution of applicant companies will be improved and strengthened, and that the quality of their products will be improved.

PART 2

CREATING

YOUR OWN

AWARDS

PROGRAM

7 Planning Your Awards Program

Association, business, recognition and charity awards take a greater or lesser degree of planning depending on their complexity.

The Primetime Emmy competition is a very complex awards process. About 100 people contribute thousands of work-hours over a period of several months just to establish the rules and procedures for a Primetime Emmy Awards competition. Then, from the time the competition begins to the announcement of the winners, nine months and tens of thousands of work-hours go into it.

At the other extreme: A relatively minor amount of planning would have gone into our hypothetical Good Egg Award. Mr. Widget could have brought it up to the board, had it approved by them and presented it to Betty from accounts receivable in a matter of days.

And yet, however complex or simple an awards program will be, the planning stage always involves four common elements:

- Rules, which define the theory or conditions of the award;

The Four Basic Elements

- Procedures, which describe the practice or implementation of the award;

- Calendar, which specifies the time frame of the awards procedures; and

- Budget, which specifies the financial frame of the awards procedures.

In creating your own awards program, you will need to address each of these four areas.

For example, note how the hypothetical Mr. Widget would incorporate all four elements in his hypothetical proposal to the board that Betty from accounts receivable get the Good Egg Award:

"From time to time we at Widget like to thank an employee who shows compassion and thoughtfulness—'subjective' traits that are not tied to the bottom line but, in their own way, are indispensable to the company."

Mr. Widget defines the theory or conditions of the award: It is not a must-give award, but is given only when appropriate; it is given to an employee; it is given as recognition for a subjective rather than an objective achievement; the achievement is supportive of the general good of the company.

"I'd like to propose for your approval that the Good Egg Award be given to Betty from accounts receivable for her proposal that the Christmas Party Fund be donated to Charity X."

The practice or implementation of the award: Mr. Widget is the designated nominator of a Good Egg; his nomination requires board approval.

"I'd like to make the presentation at our next meeting."

The time frame of the awards procedures: Mr. Widget nominates and receives approval at this meeting and specifies the next meeting as the awards presentation.

"And just for the record, the Good Egg Award is already budgeted through our General & Administrative Slush Fund."

The financial frame of the awards procedures: The Good Egg is already an approved budget item.

If you plan to establish an ongoing awards program, you will want to write it into your company's bylaws. This needn't be anything extensive.

For instance, if there were a written description of the Good Egg Award in the bylaws of the Widget Co., it might read as follows:

The Good Egg Award

The Good Egg Award was established to thank an employee who shows compassion and thoughtfulness—"subjective" traits that are not tied to the bottom line but, in their own way, are indispensable to the company.

The president of the company nominates and the board ratifies the candidate. The award is given from time to time, as appropriate.

Funding for the award comes from the General & Administrative Slush Fund.

This description of the Good Egg Award is simple

Include It in the Bylaws

and succinct. Compare it with an actual award description from the Primetime Emmys, which appears in the Academy's bylaws:

The Syd Cassyd Founders Award

The Syd Cassyd Founders Award was established to honor not only Mr. Cassyd as founder of the original ATAS, but also the award is intended to honor those Academy members who have made a significant positive impact on the Academy through their efforts and service over many years of involvement.

Members of the executive committee nominate and choose the recipient, with a final approval from the board. The executive committee's decision must be unanimous. If no candidate gets a unanimous selection, there is no award that year. No member of the executive committee is eligible for the award, nor is the immediate past president. The award is not necessarily given annually.

Note that the Emmy Award has the same elements as the hypothetical award:

- Rules: It is not a must-give award, but is given only when appropriate; it is given to a member of the Academy; it is given as a recognition for a subjective rather than an objective achievement; the achievement is supportive of the general good of the Academy.

- Procedures: Nominations come from the executive committee; no executive committee member may be a candidate; the executive committee votes on the nominations; the vote must be unanimous; the board must ratify the candidate presented by the executive committee.

- Calendar: Each annual rules book specifies that year's calendar (which generally runs from the distribution of entry forms in February to the announcement of winners in September).

- Budget: When the board approves an award, it automatically approves the funding of the award.

The same four basic elements can be found in the Baldrige Awards:

The Common Elements

- Rules: It is not a must-give award, but is given only when appropriate—with a maximum of two awards per category; Arati Prabhakar, director of NIST, has said that its purpose is "not only to recognize individual U.S. companies for their quality achievements, but also to promote quality awareness and to provide information on successful quality strategies. The major focus of the award is on results and customer satisfaction; it is not given for specific products or services."

- Procedures: Entries are made by companies; entries are initially reviewed at least 300 hours by a minimum of eight experts from the board of examiners; finalists are visited on-site by a team of six to nine examiners and an NIST official; a private-sector panel of judges reviews the site reports and makes final recommendations concerning winning companies to NIST.

- Calendar: Each annual Rules Criteria specifies that year's calendar (which generally runs from an eligibility determination in March to the announcement of winners in October).

- Budget: It is appropriated annually by the Committee on Appropriations of the U.S. House of Representatives.

Start With the Basics

As you can see, even the most complicated and labor-intensive awards program can be broken down into these four basic elements. And it can be described in just a few words.

This is the place to start when you are creating your own awards program. Before you begin to write the rules and procedures, reduce the program to its most basic elements. Capture the essence of the award first.

This will help keep you focused when you start making the myriad decisions involved in putting together an awards program—from the design of the award itself to the location of the presentation, the selection of the judges and the rules for entry.

And now, before we get down to the nitty gritty aspects of making up the rules, setting a budget and creating a timetable for your event, let's look at a few of the problems you'll want to be sure to avoid.

8   Pitfalls, Problems & Things to Avoid

Poorly designed and administered awards are dangerous for both the giver and the receiver. Every time a flawed award is given or received, it lessens the intangible value of the award and taints the acceptor.

For example, on a 1996 country music awards telecast, Garth Brooks was announced as the Entertainer of the Year. He came to the stage and said that he hadn't done much entertaining that year, and he didn't think it would be appropriate for him to get the award. Then he walked offstage, leaving the award behind like a bride that was jilted at the altar.

But, other than not attend the awards telecast, what else could he have done? Open himself to criticism for accepting an achievement award for a nonachievement? If that were the result of his acceptance, it would have been the polar opposite of what the awards were designed to accomplish.

Moreover, accepting would have been absurd, since there was nothing made extraordinary by its separation from the ordinary. What if he had accepted and later been asked by the press to comment on the entertaining that won him the Entertainer of the Year award? If he had said, "Well, I really haven't done much entertaining lately," wouldn't that have begged the questions: Why did they give the award to him? And why did he take it?

Perhaps the rules and procedures of the competition should have included some minimum requirement for Entertainer of the Year eligibility—e.g., a new album, tour, etc.—which would have disqualified Mr. Brooks. Somewhere in the details of the rules, there should have been some exclusionary clause that would have stopped the embarrassment before it happened.

Unfortunately, rules have a tendency to be written as reactions to flaws in the system, rather than as proactive guidelines that anticipate and correct the flaws.

R-E-S-P-E-C-T

Remember: Respect is hard to get and easy to lose. If the awards are not properly conceived, calendared, budgeted, judged and presented, they will not evoke respect.

Rather, they may be tainted with a generally shared sense that:

- The awards process is misadministered, and its sloppiness leads to unfairness.

- The awards process is structurally prejudicial in favor of some competitors and to the disadvantage of others.

- The competition places time and money demands on the entrants that are greater than the benefits of the awards.

- So many awards are given that the value of each one is diluted.

- The award does not represent or further the goals of its sponsoring body.

The list of perceived problems goes on and on—and as it grows, respect diminishes.

The road to Award Hell is paved with some common misperceptions about the basic principles of awards:

- **Awards have intrinsic value.** Actually, awards draw their value from the importance of the achievement they honor and the people who accept them. For example, as we've noted, the Golden Globes are given by the 85-member-strong Hollywood Foreign Press Association, which is comprised of some legitimate journalists, but also of car dealers, accountants and other part-time (and less-than-highly-respected) journalists. However, despite the iffy quality of the group that gives these awards and how they are administered, the Golden Globes have soared in value as precursors and predictors of the Oscar nominees and winners. And, however adjunct and corollary their value might be, they have enough of it to annually draw every major star in the Hollywood firmament, which in turn draws a huge television audience, which generates worldwide interest and publicity, etc., etc.
- **The value of awards is constant.** Like any commodity on any market, an award's value

fluctuates according to its assets (the importance of the achievements it honors and the people who accept them) and its productivity (the real perceived competence of the administration of the award's rules and procedures).

- **All awards are alike.** *Association awards* represent the professional purpose of their parent association and are meant to further the goals of the association and reflect its values. *Business awards* are designed to recognize outstanding achievement in business systems, services, products and quality achievement. *Recognition awards* are in-house service, sales, safety and special achievement awards meant as personal recognition with the intent of improving quality, encouraging teamwork, motivating employees, building morale, creating awareness, increasing loyalty, decreasing turnover, and enhancing the company's image in the community and among customers. And then there are *charity awards*.

- **The more awards the better (and its opposite: The fewer awards the better).** There is no constant relationship between awards quantity and quality. Too many awards dilute the value of each. Too few awards overburden the capacity of each to bear its load. Properly done awards can respond like the composer to complaints that his composition had too many or too few notes: "Not too many or too few, but just the right number."

- **Awards are reliable indicators of quality.** As they subdivide the world into the good, the bad and the rest, awards present choices for simplified decision making, and thus are a major contributor to the irony of the Information Age: the respectability given to uninformed opinion. For the most part, using awards as uninformed opinion will have minor consequences—e.g., the cost of the ticket and the boredom generated by the "must-see movie." For an example of more troubling consequences, read on.

What Is the Award For?

Parents often rely on awards to help choose books, videos and games for their children. After all, the selection available in most stores today can be overwhelming, and awards are designed to help consumers separate the extraordinary from the ordinary, right?

Yes, but it's vital to determine what the award is for. For example, a children's book may receive an award for artistic merit—the quality of its illustrations, photographs, writing or plot. But artistic merit is no guarantee that it will be a pleasant bedtime story. And it's no guarantee that the book will ascribe to the sort of family values a given consumer is trying to promote.

Chuck Colson (of Watergate fame) opined on his Internet page, dated June 24, 1996, on the misuse of prestigious awards in regard to family values:

Imagine curling up with your pajama-clad 6-year-old and reading him the latest bedtime story. You're sure the book is good, because it just won the prestigious Caldicott Award, given to the best-illustrated children's book of the year.

But if you bought one recent winner, your child might not sleep for weeks. I'm talking about a picture book called *Smoky Night*, a story about the Los Angeles riots. The book represents a trend in children's fiction to depict the chaos of modern life in all-too-graphic detail.

Smoky Night is told through the voice of a young boy named Daniel, who finds himself hurled into a nightmare world of urban violence—of gangs that roam the city, smashing windows and looting stores. Terrified adults run screaming as rioters torch Daniel's apartment building.

Boy, that ought to put your 6-year-old right to sleep.

And then there's a recent Newbery Medal winner, given by the American Library Association to what's judged the most distinguished contribution to children's literature.

Last year's winner was a book called *Walk Two Moons*. It features three children who lose their respective mothers to death, abandonment and mental illness. By the final chapter, author Sharon Creech has also killed off a beloved grandmother and a whole busload of other people.

Talk about Grimm fairy tales.

... Modern award-winners like *Smoky Night* and *Walk Two Moons* prove that parents can't judge the quality of a book by the award plastered on its cover.

Or perhaps they prove, once again, that all awards are not created equal. After all, awards for artistic merit are not the same as awards for family values.

Companies that are crafting award logos for use on winners' ads and product packaging will want to bear this in mind. A logo that mentions the award's criteria in its simplest terms will make the logo—and the award it represents—that much more valuable to consumers and to the recipient.

It has been said that imitation is the sincerest form of flattery. But it can have deleterious effects on an awards program. Consider the case of the Star Award, which bore a remarkable resemblance to the Oscar.

Beware of Cheap Imitations

Creative House, a manufacturer and distributor of advertising specialty items, had commissioned a trophy sculptor to design the Star Award in 1976, which it planned to use to honor its advertising agency client's "star" salespeople. The result was a nude, muscular male figure holding a star in its hand.

Like the Oscar, the Star Award was made of solid metal and had a shiny gold finish. Like the Oscar, its naked man stood on a circular gold cap mounted on a round base. In short, while the Star Award was a couple inches shorter than the Oscar—and held a star rather than a sword in its hand—it looked a whole lot like its far more prestigious cousin.

Had Creative House limited its distribution to a

few star salespeople at one ad agency, the resemblance probably would not have been a matter of much note (although companies are vigorously enforcing their copyrights these days).

The problem arose when Creative House began marketing and selling the award to other companies—either directly or through distributors. Most of the customers purchased the award to give to their employees. And some of those customers included theater groups, cable television companies and a film festival. Clearly, these customers were buying the award specifically because it looked like the Oscar—Creative House even noted in its ads for the Star Award that it looked like an "internationally acclaimed award given to the most talented people in the country."

This was a recipe for confusion—and confusion could devalue the Academy Award.

The Academy of Motion Picture Arts and Sciences sued Creative House for copyrighted trademark infringement in 1983. Surprisingly, a district court in California dismissed the claim. However, on appeal in 1991, the court found that there was a likelihood of confusion among consumers, which could reduce the value of an Oscar.

The court said:

The Oscar's value lies in its distinctive design, which stands as a well-recognized symbol of excellence in film. The Star Award, which is strikingly similar in appearance and was originally marketed as an award which resembles an "internationally acclaimed award," dilutes the Oscar's distinctive value.

Moreover, the Star Award is available to corporations, television stations, theater groups and any member of the general public who desires to purchase one. If the Star Award looks cheap or shoddy, or is disseminated without regard to the ultimate recipient, the Oscar's distinctive quality as a coveted symbol of excellence, which cannot be purchased from the Academy at any price, is threatened. The district court therefore erred in concluding that the Academy could not sustain a claim under the California antidilution statute.

We conclude that the Academy's sleek, muscular gold statuette known as "Oscar," which is recognized worldwide as a distinctive symbol of outstanding achievement in film, and which the Academy awards to a select group of talented individuals for the limited purpose of promoting the motion picture arts and sciences, is entitled to protection under the Copyright Act of 1976.

It's a good idea to bear this case in mind when your company is designing—or buying—a trophy for use in its award programs. You definitely don't want to infringe on someone else's copyright.

By the same token, if your company commissions a unique trophy or plaque design for use in its awards program, it's a good idea to have it copyrighted. Who knows? Your awards program may become so famous that other companies will be copying your trophies someday.

Keeping an Awards Program in Perspective

In Chapter 2, we discussed using in-house awards programs to encourage certain kinds of behavior. Clearly, you don't want to set up a program that undermines the company's long-term goals by emphasizing short-term gains, as in the case of rewarding salespeople only for new business.

You also want to be careful how your awards programs are administered. Some employees have been known to go overboard in striving to meet program goals—particularly when there is money involved. Consider the case of one company whose pursuit of safety awards landed it in court.

The firm in question, IBP Inc., is the largest producer of pork and beef in the world and employs about 29,000 workers. IBP offered financial bonuses to work sites with low worker injury and illness rates. We have mentioned several successful safety programs in other chapters—but, in this case, IBP ran into problems because of the tactics management used to keep its injury rates low. Those tactics included spying, lying and intimidation.

The situation that spawned the lawsuit involved IBP's treatment of Kevin Wilson, an employee at the company's Council Bluffs plant, who injured his back at work. Diane Arndt, a registered nurse who was IBP's manager of occupational health services, set up an appointment with a doctor who prescribed rest to treat the injury. The doctor eventually assigned Wilson to light duty at the plant.

Wilson requested a second medical opinion. The second doctor diagnosed an unstable disk and prescribed bed rest.

IBP's corporate security department then assigned a surveillance detail to Wilson to make sure he was not faking the injury. The investigators observed Wilson at home and followed him in an unmarked van. The detail reported that Wilson continued to drive his children and run errands.

Nurse Arndt then tried to persuade the doctor to release Wilson for light duty. Arndt told the doctor the company had a videotape that proved Wilson was not following his treatment regimen—although no such tape existed. The doctor discontinued treatment.

However, unlike most employees, Wilson never returned to work at IBP. He wound up settling his workers' comp claim.

Following the settlement, Wilson brought suit against IBP and Arndt, alleging that Arndt had slandered him and violated her confidential obligations as an occupational health nurse. The jury agreed—and awarded Wilson $4,000 in compensatory damages and $15 million in punitive damages. However, the court reduced the punitive damages award to $100,000. Wilson appealed, and the Iowa Supreme Court approved $2 million in punitive damages.

The Supreme Court affirmed the substantial punitive damages award because, it said, the company fostered a "climate of suspicion towards the legitimacy of injuries to workers and their treatment."

Witnesses testified that Nurse Arndt first acknowledged to Wilson's doctor that the injury was real and that he was experiencing pain. However, later, she told other nurses that he was probably faking and that she could tell there was nothing wrong with him. Witnesses also said that Arndt had an openly low opinion of workers, often characterizing them as "idiots" and "jerks" or "crybabies."

The court also implicated IBP's safety award system as a factor in its decision. The system rewarded employees of the division that had the lowest injury statistics with gifts or extra year-end bonuses.

According to the court, this safety award system gave management "strong motivation to reduce the number of lost-time days." Managers at the Council Bluffs plant not only actively sought "ultraconservative physicians" for the care of injured workers to avoid the cost of medical treatment, but the company also made injured workers punch in at work and then sent them home, allowing the injury to be recorded as a full work day. Nurses, including Arndt, entered incorrect information in the computer system used to determine whether a given injury was recordable under OSHA regulations. This resulted in many injuries being erroneously classified as nonrecordable.

Besides spying, the company also employed other methods for coercing employees to return to work after injuries. Workers who did not want to cooperate with the planned medical treatment were assigned by Arndt to a light-duty job: watching gauges in the rendering plant while being subjected to an atrocious smell from hog remains, which were boiled into fertilizers, and from blood draining into tanks.

In short, the court found that IBP exhibited "willful and wanton disregard for the rights and safety of Wilson." The "outrageous conduct" of IBP and its managers warranted punitive damages of $2 million.

While IBP managers put employees at risk in pursuit of an award, the federal Labor Department put the reputation of its awards program at risk by rewarding a company that was simultaneously being sanctioned by the state in which it was doing business.

Just hours after Harry Singh & Sons, a tomato farmer, received the Regional Agricultural Employer of the Year award for improving the working and living conditions of farm workers in 1996, a California labor inspector tried to serve the Singh family with a lawsuit. As it turned out, the supposedly exemplary employer owed somewhere in the vicinity of $1 million in unpaid overtime wages.

"I wish it were funny, but it isn't," Claudia Smith, regional counsel for California Rural Legal Assistance, which first brought the complaint about alleged overtime violations to the state in 1993, told the Associated Press.

The lawsuit, filed in the spring of 1995, claims workers for the Oceanside, California, tomato grower put in as many as 82½ hours a week, but were paid a flat $4.25 an hour, the minimum wage, according to Smith. While farm workers are exempt from federal overtime rules, California law does require that they get time-and-a-half for more than 60 hours of work in a week.

Jose Millan, assistant state labor commissioner, said he was shocked his federal counterparts would go ahead with the award presentation, despite the state's overtime suit.

Clearly, it pays to investigate a company before you decide to honor it with an award. A little legwork can save a lot of face for the award giver and the recipient—and save the award's reputation.

9

Making Up the Rules

Rules define the theory or conditions of an award, and by doing so they suggest the type of individual who is eligible to receive that award. Therefore, no matter how simple or how complicated your awards program will be, the place to start when you are writing the rules is by deciding to whom you would like to give an award.

This sounds simple enough. But there are many things to consider. For an in-house awards program, will you reward loyalty, innovation or determination? Or will you reward income generation? Will the award go only to a full-time employee, or can part-timers, temps and freelancers qualify? Can a team qualify on the basis of a group effort, or will the award go to individuals only?

For outside awards programs, will the award go only to suppliers who do a certain amount of business with your company? Do they have to have worked with you for a set period of time? Do they have to be based in the United States?

For association awards, will the competition be open to members only, or can nonmembers win?

In addition, you'll need to decide if people will be allowed to win the award several years in a row. Also, will you allow more than one person (or company) to win an award in the event of a tie, or will there be some sort of runoff vote or tiebreaker?

Obviously, there are many issues to consider. And the more issues you clarify up front, the less potential for problems down the road.

Who Will Qualify?

Sometimes, it seems obvious who is or is not an eligible candidate for an award. In the case of the Emmys, who would be eligible for the Outstanding Individual Achievement in Directing award? The person suggested by the rules—in this case, the title of the category—would be a person credited as the "director."

Who would be an eligible candidate for the Outstanding Individual Achievement in Choreography award? It would be a person credited as the "choreographer."

But eligibility can have its complications. Consider who might be eligible to win the Outstanding Individual Achievement in Picture Editing Emmy:

- Would it be the picture editor who contributes to the creative decisions about how to piece the raw footage together into a coherent whole—the so-called "off line editor"?

- Or would it be the picture editor who follows the off line editor with the physical assembly of the designated pieces—the so-called "on line editor"?

- Or would it be the picture editor known as the "clip editor"—the person who takes old footage and re-edits it into a new context where needed on some shows (e.g., a "Best of ..." special that includes old footage)?

Questions of eligibility should be answered in the rules—i.e., at the point at which the definition and conditions of the award are established. What do the Emmy rules say about the eligibility of picture editors?

They disallow from eligibility both the on line and clip editors, leaving only the off line editor the opportunity to enter, compete and win an Emmy. This is because the off line editor generally takes the greatest creative responsibility for the structure of the program, and is therefore the *ideal candidate* for an Emmy.

Ideal is shorthand for what is a generally-agreed-upon ideal of fairness. Rules embody the ideal and, in most instances, they deliver it. But there are special circumstances in which rules deliver an unfair verdict. The picture editor situation is a case in point.

During the 1993 Primetime competition, the Academy received a Picture Editing entry for "Bob Hope: The First 90 Years." The entry listed three off line editors. Subsequently, six clip editors petitioned for eligibility alongside the off line editors. Since most of the show was made up of footage pieced together by the clip editors, they argued that theirs was the special achievement that caught the attention of the voters and would significantly contribute to a picture editing nomination. To deny them Emmy eligibility would be patently unfair. The three off line editors agreed and backed their appeal.

The Exception to the Rule

The Editors Peer Group Executive Committee—the arbiter of such eligibility disputes—agreed that theirs was an unusual and major contribution to the completed program, and that they should receive eligibility. (They were nominated, but the Emmy went to the picture editors of a David Copperfield special.)

When you are writing your rules, you will want to consider as many eventualities as possible. But you also will need to make a provision to consider other candidates that don't quite fit the rules structure, à la the Emmy Awards committee.

Special Case Restrictions

"Special case" restrictions on eligibility are found throughout awards competitions. Here are some recurring categories:

- quantity restrictions;

- multiple application restrictions;

- future eligibility restrictions;

- principal identity restrictions;

- prior achievement restrictions;

- time frame restrictions;

- age restrictions; and

- moral suitability restrictions.

What follows are a number of examples of these category restrictions that should give you options on how to customize the scope of your rules. If you were to use them all in a hypothetical Bigfoot Walk Across America competition, you might limit eligibility to:

- persons with a 12 or larger shoe size (quantity)
- who have not competed in the Bigfoot Walk Across the Klondike competition (multiple application) and
- may only enter in the year their feet first become a size 12 (future eligibility).
- They must be of Inuit heritage (principal identity) and
- have been a finalist in the Nome Marathon (prior achievement)
- during the past two years (time frame).
- They can be no more than 18 years old (age restriction) and
- cannot have been convicted of littering (moral suitability).

Quantity Restrictions

An example of a quantity restriction in the Primetime Emmys is the requirement that a minimum of two-thirds of the sets and locales of a series submission for art direction must be new in the current eligibility year. If, for example, the art director for *Seinfeld* did not have a current episode that had two-thirds new sets and locales (and not just the apartment, diner and street scenes recurring from the prior season), he or she would be restricted from entering the competition.

Another example is the Motion Picture Academy's Oscar for Visual Effects, which is open to the "primary individuals—not to exceed four in number—directly involved with, and principally responsible for, the visual effects achieved."

But what if there are more than four people who made equally important contributions to the achievement? Numerical eligibility restrictions always run the risk of arbitrarily excluding a worthy individual—as evidenced in the 1997 Oscars.

The January 3, 1997, issue of *Daily Variety* reported, "The pyrotechnics surrounding the Academy of Motion Picture Arts & Sciences' visual effects awards this year won't all be on the screen. A pair of visual effects workers on two major features are publicly charging that their names have been unfairly excluded from Oscar ballots." One of the excluded individuals was "appalled" by her exclusion from the list, and the other felt it would cause his professional reputation to suffer.

Those who were forced by the numerical restriction to make the decisions that excluded the pair were equally upset. Said one, "We agonized over this. ... There are five very deserving people. ... It's just very difficult for us to break it down any further than five names."

All the problems prompted the chairman of the Academy committee overseeing the entries to pledge to change the process next year.

Quantity restrictions also can refer to the number of employees at a company. For instance, suppose the Widget Co. has a subsidiary that does nothing but research and development. It is a separate entity from the parent, with its own organizational chart, administrative manual and annual report. The managers of the subsidiary wish to enter the Malcolm Baldrige Awards competition. Because the parent company is a manufacturing firm, they enter as a Manufacturing Subsidiary. Their entry is rejected, with the following explanation of a quantity restriction:

> In the Baldrige Awards, where Manufacturing is a category of competition open to companies or their subsidiaries, a complication arises with the entry from the Widget subsidiary because of the rule that the parent company has to have more than 500 full-time employees in order for its subsidiary company to be eligible. A manufacturing company with less than 500 full-time employees must enter, because of its size, in the Small Business category, which does not allow separate entries from subsidiaries.

Because the Widget Co. only has 300 full-time employees, its subsidiary cannot make a Manufacturing Subsidiary entry.

Some other variations on quantity restrictions:

- The Contemporary Record Society's National Competition for Composers allows entrants to submit any number of works, but each entry is limited to performances that do not exceed nine players.

- The ACSA/Otis Elevator International Student Design Competition is limited to designs for elevators in mid-rise housing—i.e., buildings that are generally between two and 10 stories tall. High-rise elevator designs are not eligible.

- The Spirit Awards for independent films must demonstrate "economy of means" (i.e., a low budget).

- The Cable Television Administration and Marketing Society's Awards for Excellence in Marketing and Advertising stipulates quantity restrictions for each of its three categories of competition: 1) regional markets with more than 250,000 subscribers; 2) less than 250,000 subscribers; and 3) less than 60,000 subscribers.

Multiple Application Restrictions

In the Baldrige Awards, the multiple application restriction takes the form of a rule that "a subsidiary and its parent company may not both apply for awards in the same year."

In the Primetime Emmys, it disallows the entry of a single program in more than one category. For example, although *The Simpsons* is both a comedy series and an animated program, it must choose to enter in either the Outstanding Comedy Series or Outstanding Animated Program (One Hour or Less) category. It cannot enter in both.

Sometimes multiple entries are allowed, but only up to a point. For instance, in the Pulitzer Prizes, exhibits in the public service, cartoon and photography categories are limited to 20 articles, cartoons or pictures. In the remaining categories, they are limited to 10 articles or editorials—except for feature writing, which is limited to three articles of more than 1,500 words or five articles of 1,500 words or less.

In the Baldrige Awards, the future eligibility restriction precludes a company or its subsidiaries that have won an award from competing again for a period of five years.

Companies may apply for the Japan Quality Medal five years or more (including the award year) after they receive a Deming Prize. When it has been determined that an applicant company's implementation of companywide quality control has improved substantially beyond when it won the Deming Prize, the company is awarded the medal.

In the Primetime Emmys, a musician may enter his or her Main Title Theme only in the year that it is originally aired.

You may want to limit the future eligibility of winners in an effort to "share the wealth." Or you may prefer to allow those who are deserving to win over and over again to avoid penalizing them—and to set them up as examples for others.

Sometimes, it is tough to know how to categorize people, companies and products. A principal identity restriction—or set of rules—can help.

For instance, there is a possibility that a business might be engaged in both manufacturing and service. Therefore, it would appear to be eligible for either the Baldrige Manufacturing category or the Service category. However, what would seem to be a matter of discretion for the entrant is ruled out by a restriction that establishes the *principal identity* of the company as that which has the larger percentage of sales.

Split identity becomes an eligibility complication in the Primetime Emmys, as well, with programs that are a combination of live action and animation. As with the above example, the principal identity question is resolved according to which part is predominant.

A variation on principal identity restrictions is the notion of one's eligibility being based on a personal trait or characteristic. For instance, the Lefthanders of the Year Awards are limited to southpaws who have made a significant achievement during the previous year as a public, entertainment, music or sports personality. The National Amputee Golf Association's Champion Award and the Bald Is Beautiful Award are other examples.

Profession is another type of principal identity. To enter the Pro Rodeo Clown of the Year competition as a Coors "Man in the Can" contestant, one has to be a Pro Rodeo Cowboys Association "barrelman"—i.e., a rodeo clown who works the animals in the open ring with only a barrel for sanctuary.

Similarly, the World Modeling Association's International Fashion Model Award is open only to people who are models, and the Driver of the Year Award is open only to competition auto racers. (While the latter award is open to racers of all varieties, until John Force won it in 1996, it had gone only to road and oval-track racers—never to anyone whose principal identity was nitro-fuel funny car driver.)

Other principal identities that figure in eligibility restrictions are race and religion. For example, the Metropolitan Life Foundation Award Program for Academic Excellence in Medicine is restricted to members of minority groups that are considered under-represented in medicine by the Association of American Medical Colleges, and the Aleph Award is given to recognize Jewish study on the part of Cub Scouts of the Jewish faith.

For eligibility in the Academy of Canadian Cinema and Television's Gemini Awards, "Canadian content" must be established. In addition, the producers must be Canadian citizens, at least 75 percent of all production and post-production costs must be paid to Canadians or for services provided in Canada, and a number of key creative people must be Canadian.

Similarly, candidates for Sunday's Evening Standard British Film Awards, one of Britain's premier annual cinema events, must be British films. And the Whitbread Prize is open only to writers who have lived in Great Britain or Ireland for three or more years.

Prior Achievement

Some awards require that you've already won. For instance, associations may require that you win one or more regional awards before you can compete for a national honor.

Among iris growers, the competition for the Clarence G. White Medal is open only to those specimens that have already received an award of merit, as well as an Honorable Mention Award, by the American Iris Society.

Contestants in the American Crossword Puzzle competition are assigned to divisions based on prior achievements. Division B is for contestants who have not finished within the top 10 percent in a sanctioned tournament in the last three years. Division C is for contestants who have not finished within the top 20 percent, and so on, down to Division E for those who have not finished in the top 65 percent.

Two famous variations on prior achievement restrictions are horse racing's Triple Crown Championship (for a horse that swept the Kentucky Derby, Preakness Stakes and Belmont Stakes) and major league baseball's Triple Crown Batting Championship (for most hits, most runs batted in and highest batting average).

A similar restriction applies for eligibility in the Community Action Network's Annual Media & Corporate Awards. It only recognizes solutions to social problems that have a media-reported history—i.e., they must have been reported in either print or broadcast media, including corporate newsletters and annual reports.

Time Frame Restrictions

Another kind of restriction is time. Although generally used to define the eligibility period (e.g., the shows that are eligible for the Primetime Emmys that will be awarded in September 1997 must have aired originally during the period June 1, 1996, through May 31, 1997), time restrictions also can be applied in other ways.

For instance:

- The Canadian Cardiovascular Society Research Achievement Award limits eligibility to those investigations that have been conducted within the last five years.

- Oscar eligibility generally is limited to films that premiered during the calendar year.

- To be eligible for the Phoenix Book Award, a children's book must have been published 20 years prior to the entry year.

Sometimes, time restrictions can get more complicated, as with the Edgar Allan Poe Awards (the Edgars). Candidates are eligible if they were copyrighted and published or shown for the first time in the United States during the eligibility calendar year. But what if an author copyrighted his or her mystery novel in 1984, then was unable to find a publisher and make the entry until 1996? Would the copyright disqualify the book? Edgar rules say no—the date of publication takes precedence over the copyright date.

Age Restrictions

Age restrictions can get sticky in a business setting, but they have their place. For instance, the Specialty Equipment Marketing Association, the national trade group for the automotive aftermarket, gives an award to the Young Executive of the Year, who must be 35 or younger.

The Congressional Awards recognize American youth for their voluntary public service and personal excellence, and are limited to candidates 14 through 23 years of age. The Bronze Award is for individuals at least 14 but not yet 17. Silver Award eligibility is limited to individuals at least 17 but not yet 20. And the Gold Award is for 18- to 23-year-olds.

The Australian/Vogel book awards are for authors under 35 years of age.

Moral Suitability

Moral suitability is an area that many companies may not get into. But if you will be offering awards to video game creators, computer program creators, artists of any type or several other groups, you may need to incorporate rules concerning moral issues. These could refer to pornographic or violent content, nudity, political orientation, sexual orientation or any number of other criteria.

For instance, program entries in the Shanghai Television Festival may be excluded if they extol violence or are pornographic.

(While we live in a democratic nation, there is nothing that says you cannot create whatever rules you deem appropriate for your awards program. However, bear in mind that some rules may lead you to court someday.)

An interesting reversal of the usual way that moral suitability restricts eligibility is found with the John Huston Award for Artists Rights. As the *Hollywood Reporter* noted in a series of articles in February 1997, in the Berne Treaty, the international standard for intellectual copyright protection, there is a "so-called moral rights clause that gives the 'author' of a work of art the right to 'object to any distortion, mutilation or other modification of, or other derogatory action in relation to the said work which would be prejudicial to his honor or reputation. The United States signed the Berne Treaty in 1989, but does not recognize the right of film artists to object to the mutilation of their work. Under U.S. law, the owner of a film's copyright [generally the studio or production company] is the 'author' of the film."

But if the film maker is a director whose black and white picture has been colorized and shown on television—as was the case with John Huston's *The Asphalt Jungle*, which was colorized by Turner Entertainment for France's Channel Five—or so edited for television that it is rendered incoherent (as in Milos Forman's *Hair*), he or she may be eligible for the Huston Award. Directors who *have not* suffered the loss of their moral right to have their work seen as they intended it are excluded from eligibility for this award.

In a more traditional take on moral suitability exclusions, this time of the unwritten variety, the *New York Times* reported that legendary film maker Elia Kazan has repeatedly been denied lifetime achievement awards from both the Los Angeles Film Critics Association and the American Film Institute. The reason for this "sustained censure," according to the paper, is that he "informed on his old friends in the Communist Party when he was summoned to testify before the House Un-American Activities Committee in 1952."

The *Times'* editorial opinion, published in January 1997, said, "Not only did he name names, causing lasting damage to individual careers, but he lent his prestige and moral authority to what was essentially an immoral process, a brief but nevertheless damaging period of officially sponsored hysteria that exacted a huge toll on individual lives, on free speech and on democracy."

All that having been said, the *Times* noted: "His artistic record is far more impressive than most of those honored by the Film Critics Association and the Film Institute. It is artistry, not politics, that the awards are supposed to honor. For Mr. Kazan's long-ago failure to speak out against blacklisting, Hollywood's arbiters continue to indulge their own form of blacklisting. This is not progress."

When Lawyers Get Involved

In this litigious day and age, one can never be too careful when drafting the rules. If at all possible, go through an industry magazine or directory and look at as many of the possible entrants as you can. Try to imagine all the possible scenarios, and consider whether they fit into any of the categories you have created.

If a number of them do not, you may be asking for headaches. Just ask the organizers of the Tony Awards.

In 1995, Jackie Mason sued the organizers for their refusal to categorize his one-man topical comedy *Jackie Mason: Politically Incorrect* as a "play" eligible for a Tony Award in the 1993-94 Broadway season. The comedian demanded $75 million in compensatory and punitive damages—plus costs.

The Antoinette Perry ("Tony") Awards are awarded annually for excellence in the theater in certain categories of achievement. Eligibility is determined by the Tony Awards Administration Committee, a self-governing body established by Tony Award Productions. The committee is comprised of 24 individuals designated by the American Theatre Wing, the League of American Theaters and Producers, the Dramatists Guild, the Actor's Equity Association, United Scenic Artists, and the Society of Stage Directors and Choreographers.

In his decision in the lawsuit, Judge Herman Cahn discussed the relevant rules (which should provide some ideas for rule-drafting readers):

Tony Rule 4(a) lists the categories in which "regular" Tonys may be awarded. Most category names specifically refer to either a "play" or a "musical," e.g., "Best Play," "Best Musical," "Best Performance

Chapter 9—Making Up the Rules

by a Leading Actress in a Play," etc. A number do not contain those terms (e.g., simply "Best Costume Design," "Best Choreography"), but the omission is apparently not significant. Other rules also contain references to "plays or musicals," clearly implying that those are the only types of productions eligible for regular Tonys. However, Rules 4(c) and (d) provide for discretionary "Special Tony Awards," which may be granted to "a theatrical event ... which does not fit into any existing Tony Award category," as well as for "lifetime achievement in the theatre."

Tony Rule 2 sets forth the six requirements a production must satisfy to be eligible in the "various categories." The committee must determine that the entrant is "a legitimate theatrical production," but definitions of "play" or "musical" as used in the "various categories" are not provided. Also, as is relevant here, Rule 2(v) requires the producer of a production seeking consideration to invite and provide free tickets to all eligible Tony voters, and to certify in writing to the committee that the invitations were extended in the manner and number prescribed by the rules. The remaining eligibility requirements relate to minimum theater size and opening date cutoffs.

Regardless of a show's eligibility, the committee still retains discretion to determine "whether a sufficient number of eligible candidates exist in quality or quantity to merit the granting of an award in the applicable category for the current season," Tony Rule 2(j)(A). Similarly, it has "sole discretion to reduce the number of nominees to fewer than four ... in a particular category for the current season." Finally, Rule 1(a) provides that "all decisions of the [committee] concerning eligibility for the awards and all other matters relating to their administration and presentation ... shall be final."

The court went on to point out:

Mason has presented one-man topical comedy performances on Broadway since at least the 1986-87 season, when he starred in *The World According to Jackie Mason*. He accepted a Special Tony Award for "Excellence in the Theatre" that year, but the production was apparently deemed ineligible for a regular Tony because it was not considered a play or musical. Mason did not challenge that determination, nor a similar one made concerning his show *Jackie Mason: Brand New* in 1990.

Jackie Mason: Politically Incorrect opened on April 5, 1994. On April 7, 1994, the committee met and determined that the show was not eligible for a Tony because, ... like his previous productions, it was not a play or a musical. Mason did not object or take other action between that date and the presentation ceremony on June 12, 1994. The instant suit, for monetary damages only, was commenced on August 4, 1994.

In considering the case, Hahn wrote:

The courts, of course, do not usually decide who is eligible to receive a Tony, or to whom one should be awarded. This suit could be dismissed out of hand if Mason were simply complaining that his

Chapter 9—Making Up the Rules

show "deserved" to win a nomination or trophy on its merits. As noted in a related context, most honors are alike in that some individual or committee must review what someone has accomplished and make a subjective judgment of whether that conduct is deserving of reward or recognition. Inherent in such a system is the possibility of error. If Paul Newman (*The Verdict*) wins the Academy Award instead of Dustin Hoffman (*Tootsie*), who is to say that he is really more deserving?

The precise issue here, however, is one step removed from the highly subjective process of selecting a Tony winner. It concerns the corporate defendants' application of the internal, published threshold requirements regarding eligibility, not the ultimate determination of which shows are "better" or "best." Defendants' status as the conferrers of a highly publicized entertainment industry award does not immunize them from the normal rules of corporate or organizational governance, although the scope of judicial review of such private sector decisions is extraordinarily narrow.

... All that is left, then, is the question of whether defendants had authority to decide that Mason's production was not a play. They most certainly did. The power to make final determinations regarding all matters of eligibility was expressly granted to the Committee by the Tony Rules, as was the discretion to award no Tonys at all. Further inquiry as to the wisdom of their action is precluded.

In an effort to raise the specter of bad faith, Mason avers that Lily Tomlin received a regular Tony ("Leading Actress in a Play") in 1986 for *The Search for Signs of Intelligent Life in the Universe*. That solitary example is insufficient to demonstrate that plaintiff was the victim of discriminatory enforcement of the rules. ...

Moreover, defendants have provided numerous examples of comedy routines which were disqualified because they were not plays (Spaulding Gray's *Gray's Anatomy*, 1993-94; Victor Borge, 1989-90; Robert Klein, 1988-89; Mort Sahl, 1987-88; Whoopi Goldberg, 1984-86) and musicians whose shows were not deemed musicals (Michael Feinstein, 1987-88, 1988-89, 1990-91; Barry Manilow, 1988-89; Mandy Patinkin, 1989-90; Stephanie Mills, 1989-90; Harry Connick Jr., 1990-91; Tommy Tune, 1992-93; Raffi, 1992-93; Tony Bennett, 1992-93; Jackson Browne, 1993-94), demonstrating a rationality and consistency that would pass muster regardless of the burden of proof or standard of review.

Clearly, when you are crafting the rules for your awards program, it is imperative that those rules state that you or your judges have complete discretionary control over who is or is not eligible, as well as all other aspects of the awards program. And it is imperative that you follow the rules in a consistent manner, making exceptions only where you deem them clearly in the interest of fairness.

When you make exceptions to the rules on a regular basis, it can be painful for all parties involved to go back to actually following the rules. Consider the sort of predicament that the Golden Globe Awards found itself in at the end of 1996:

In February of 1996, the Hollywood Foreign Press Association issued its rules and entry forms. The rules stipulated that a feature film had to play in Los Angeles for at least a week prior to the end of the year in order to qualify for eligibility in the 1997 awards—i.e., no movie would be eligible that debuted after Christmas Day.

Unfortunately, the rule generally had not been enforced in the past. The *Los Angeles Times* reported that the 1996 nominations had included one for Brad Pitt in *12 Monkeys* (which opened on December 27, 1995—two days after the deadline), one for Susan Sarandon in *Dead Man Walking* (which opened on December 26, 1995—one day after the deadline) and one for Ian McKellen in *Richard III* (which also opened on December 26). In prior years, *Fried Green Tomatoes* (1991), *Lorenzo's Oil* (1992) and *In the Name of the Father* (1993) had missed the deadline but had received several nominations each.

Phil Berk, the president of the Golden Globes, was quoted by the *Times* as saying that the deadline "had been overlooked" in the past, but would now be observed in order to "strengthen the credibility of the organization" and its awards.

That was cold comfort to the studios, which assumed the rule would once again be ignored—and, in order to avoid the Christmas crowding caused by the plethora of holiday films, scheduled their releases for after December 25. "We planned a strategy for so long that we're very disappointed at this turn of events," said a spokesman for Grammercy Pictures, which was scheduling the release of two of its biggest pictures of the year (*I'm Not Rappaport* and *The Portrait of a Lady*) for December 26 and 27, respectively. "If a change was to be made, why not tell us in January [of 1997] and make it relevant to the coming year?"

Mr. Berk responded that "they knew of the rule back in February when we sent out the [entry] forms."

But who knew it would be enforced?

Protect Your Company

Just as companies cannot expect to go unscathed if they have capricious hiring and promotion procedures, they cannot expect to go unscathed if they are capricious when it comes to their awards programs. By now, it should be clear that an inconsistent reading of the rules definitely can lead to trouble.

If you aren't entirely convinced, just ask New England Telephone (NET). The company was sued by a former employee, William J. Hodgkins Jr., for implying that he would get a substantial financial award, offering a smaller one, then later refusing to pay anything above an initial installment of $5,000.

Hodgkins' confusion and concern were understandable. He had retired from the company earlier than he would have if he had not expected to receive $50,000 from NET—the maximum payout from the Ideas at Work (IAW) program.

NET's employee suggestion program was designed to encourage and reward employees who offered ideas that produced savings or increased profits for NET—the kind of program many companies offer these days. According to the program's rules, it "rewards the people who come up with ideas the company uses by paying the originators 15 percent of the savings or earnings from the first year of implementation—up to a limit of $50,000."

It provides for Initial Awards of 15 percent (a minimum of $75 and a maximum of $5,000) of the estimated net savings or profits for one year on so-called "tangible ideas," and Special Merit Awards of up to 15 percent of the actual savings or profits produced by the idea in its first year of implementation. According to a handbook that NET supplied to employees, "All tangible ideas which were awarded an Initial Award will be reevaluated one year from the date of implementation to determine the actual savings or profits."

Hodgkins, who worked for NET in Maine from 1956 until February 1992, came up with an idea that would reduce the cost of changing telephone service for certain "multisubscribers," such as dormitories and nursing homes. He submitted his idea to the IAW program on April 20, 1989.

Based on his own managerial expertise, Hodgkins conducted a study and concluded that the idea would save NET money—and, therefore, NET would implement the idea, evaluate it under the IAW program and grant him 15 percent of the first year's savings. Based on his knowledge of NET's operations and costs, Hodgkins expected to receive the maximum award under the IAW program: $50,000.

His expectations seemed to be confirmed by NET. The company's initial evaluation in August 1990 reported that Hodgkins' suggestion was "an excellent idea to move the company forward in its goal of automated provisioning." It rewarded him for his idea with the maximum Initial Award of $5,000 in September 1990. NET even announced that his idea had been adopted in the company's house newsletter, stating that it "earned for its suggester a Tangible Award of 15 percent of its estimated savings."

But, in September 1992, NET manager Philip DuBois told Hodgkins that NET had awarded him $17,500 for his idea.

Hodgkins was shocked. Based on his expectation of receiving the maximum $50,000 award, he had retired a few months earlier, in February 1992.

The company agreed to reevaluate the award.

This is where things get a bit sticky for NET—and really sticky for Hodgkins. In August 1993, NET informed Hodgkins that he would not receive a Special Merit Award. According to the company's reevaluation report, NET could not quantify the savings associated *exclusively* with Hodgkins' idea because other innovations had produced the same results.

Hodgkins again appealed the company's decision and a second reevaluation was performed, which arrived at the same conclusion. To make matters worse, given the passage of time, measuring savings had been rendered impossible by the destruction of cost records.

At this point, Hodgkins brought suit in district court, seeking damages incurred in reliance on statements made by NET, as well as the additional $45,000 of award money he expected, plus money for income taxes, which NET had agreed to pay on any IAW program award amount.

However, Hodgkins had submitted his idea to the IAW program by signing a submission form in which he agreed to abide by the rules of the program as laid out on the reverse side of the form. According to the court, the rules stated:

> that NET had the sole, exclusive and complete discretion and right to determine the terms, policy, structure, operation and administration of the program, including the right: .... e) To determine the method for calculating the amount of any award. f) To determine the amount of any award granted. g) To determine the person entitled to receive any award. h) To determine the extent, if any, of the application, implementation or use of an idea. The same documents also provided that "the decisions of the company concerning the terms, policy, structure, operation or administration of the program are within the sole and exclusive discretion of the company and are final, binding and conclusive."

The district court granted summary judgment in favor of NET on all counts. Not surprisingly, Hodgkins appealed.

The appeals court wrote:

> The district court decided that the IAW program formed part of Hodgkins' contract of employment with NET. The district court also found that the provision of the IAW program that states that "all ideas which result in Initial Awards for tangible ideas shall receive consideration for a Special Merit Award" was "clearly enforceable." However, the district court found crucial the IAW program's

express condition that NET had "the sole, exclusive and complete discretion and right to determine the terms, policy, structure, operation and administration of the program." The district court pointed to the IAW program Submission Form, which, along with allocating such discretion to NET, provides that NET has the right "to determine the method for evaluating ideas which are submitted" and "to determine the method for calculating the amount of any award to be granted." As a result, the district court found an enforceable contract—one which it found NET did not breach.

On appeal, Hodgkins argues that the IAW program is severable from his employment contract, and that by accepting his submission and implementing his idea, NET was bound to pay him if it was successful. Hodgkins also contends that while there was no explicit reasonableness requirement in Hodgkins' contract with NET, other terms in the contract substitute for it. Under this reading of the contract, Hodgkins asserts that a genuine issue of material fact persisted with respect to whether NET breached the contract.

... As a result, we must look beyond the mere wording of the agreement. ... Viewing the facts in the best light for Hodgkins, the general purpose of the IAW program agreement appears fairly straightforward. An employee suggestion plan such as the IAW program is intended to reward ideas and promote more active employee participation in the productive process. ... These programs give employees incentives in the form of rewards to work harder and generate possible improvements. ... At the same time, the clauses in the employment contract and the proposal plan document must be upheld to protect the company's interests. ... Among those interests is the ability of the employer to quickly resolve instances where the suggestion involved may provide benefits that are difficult or impossible to quantify.

Nonetheless, the court said:

Given its policies of generally informing its employees when one of them received an award, the context in which NET made its promise did not allow it to refuse to pay awards arbitrarily at its discretion. If NET refused to pay awards, then the IAW program in the future would not provide incentives to employees to suggest improvements. Future improvements depended, and still depend, on current payment of awards.

When all was said and done, the court did indeed find that NET could not simply offer Hodgkins a $17,500 Special Award and then change its mind. The appeals court then remanded the case to the lower court for further proceedings.

Is There a Judge and Jury in Your Future?

Obviously, nobody sets up an awards program so that they will land in court, battling it out over who is eligible and how much they deserve to win.

The best way to stay out of court is to determine who is eligible to win your awards, then set hard and fast rules, along with some mechanism to consider exceptions when necessary. Make the rules clear to everyone involved. And abide by your own rules, enforcing them in a consistent manner.

Then you can choose your own judge and maybe even your own jury. After all, someone is going to have to decide who will win those awards.

I'll Be the Judge of That

Once you have determined who you want to reward and for what, it's time to determine exactly how your awards program will be judged—and by whom.

For instance, will the competition have one judge, a few judges or an open-ended number? If your company is starting an awards program, will you make a unilateral decision, will your board of directors vote, or will you have employees—or your customers—do the voting?

You may even want to initiate a two-step judging process, in which employees or customers or supervisors submit nominations, then the board of directors or a panel of judges makes the final decisions.

The other big decision concerns the judging criteria. Will you create a competitive program, in which only one candidate can win in a particular category? Or will it be a non-competitive program, in which you may give out several awards—or you may not give out any?

We'll begin this chapter by considering the characteristics of competitive and non-competitive awards processes. Then we'll take a look at the judges themselves.

What Makes a Competition?

There is a general similarity among the participants in a competition. A race pitting a horse against a duck and a nitro funny car would be a curiosity, but it would not be what is generally thought of as a competition. "Like vs. like" makes for a competition.

All horses in a race are alike in a general equestrian way—and most have demonstrated similar abilities. This makes it a fair and interesting competition.

But in any given race on any given day, the first one across the line is unlike the others in the most important way—it's faster. Competitions such as horse races are structured to produce a single winner. There is always a possibility of a photo-finish tie, but this is the exception to the rule that a head-to-head competition produces a single winner.

Breaking from the starting line and galloping toward the pole, the first horse across the finish line wins the race. It doesn't make any difference if the winner takes 59:00 minutes to run a mile and the second horse takes 59:01.

In competitions, there is no *minimum, objective standard* of performance. All that matters in the ranking of win, place and show are the competitors' *relative performances* in the race being run.

The Miss America pageant and other beauty contests are similar to horse races in this regard. The contestants do not compete against some idealized standard of beauty. Rather, they compete against other contestants—and their ranking is therefore based on their relative beauty.

Advantage in competitions is given or received because of the competitors' errors. A horse may be lagging behind in second place with no chance of winning the race, when suddenly the lead jockey makes an error and turns his horse into the rail. By the time the lead horse has recovered, the second-place horse has passed him and won.

Horses do not win every race they run because of objective and subjective variables. Some horses run well on a muddy track; some under the guidance of a particular jockey; and others just because they are having a good day. The uncertainty is what makes a horse race (and a competition).

Category competition in the Primetime Emmy Awards is much like a horse race. Entrants come forward in "like vs. like" fields of competition that are designed to produce a single winner. The top five vote-getters in the nominating phase of the competition "take the lead." And the highest vote-getter among the nominees "wins the race" in the "final stretch" of the judging panels.

A Competitive Awards Process

The winner simply garners the most votes. He or she does not have to achieve a minimum percentage or number of votes to win.

As in a horse race, advantage may be given or received because of an error. For instance, nominees must select an episode for the judges to use while making their decision. But say an actress who has been nominated for her very funny performances in a comedy series chooses to send the judges a "Very Special Episode"—Hollywoodese for a "serious issue" episode (e.g., Major Dad gets orders for the Gulf War or Edith Bunker is raped)—because she thinks "dramatic" is more

Emmy-worthy than "comic." Her error is that dramatic is appropriate for dramatic programming, but she was nominated for comedy. The judges expect her to be "comedic," and that is what they are going to vote for.

Also, as in a horse race, because of the objective and subjective variables inherent in both the entrant's achievement and the evaluation of the judges, it is never certain who will win the Emmy.

Other examples of competitive awards processes include the Malcolm Baldrige Award for Health Care. To make sure the competition is between "like vs. like," the category is limited to organizations that are "primarily engaged in furnishing medical, surgical and other health services to persons. Examples of health care organizations include, but are not limited to, hospitals, HMOs, nursing homes, health care practitioner offices, home health agencies and dialysis centers. Organizations that do not directly provide health services to persons, such as social service agencies, health insurance companies or medical/dental laboratories, are not eligible."

Competitors in the Computerworld Smithsonian Awards Program also are divided into 10 categories of "likes." Each is judged on its visionary use of information technology (IT) to produce positive social, economic and educational changes. Although there are entries from "unlikes" as diverse as a jeans manufacturer and a pharmaceutical company, each Business and Related Services candidate fulfills the criteria of using IT to "create positive change in our society through technology." For instance:

- Custom jeans measurements are transmitted from retail stores to the factory, where an individualized pair of jeans is sewn for delivery to the customer, improving the overall fit to customer needs (Custom Clothing Technology Corp./Levi Strauss).

- On-line management and record-keeping of more than a billion pharmaceutical prescriptions lowers cost, increases customer satisfaction and supports analysis of drug effectiveness (PCS Health Systems Inc.).

Similarly, in the Education and Academia category, Harvard Medical School's palmtop computers transform the ability of medical students to access and utilize information, while Carnegie Mellon University's remote computer access to laboratory instruments allows undergraduate students to conduct actual experiments at any time and from any location.

In the Science category, "likes" include Carnegie Mellon University's automated light microscopes that acquire, process, analyze, display and archive four-dimensional image data on the chemical dynamics that are responsible for the functioning of living cells and the University of Arizona's supercomputer simulation of the ventricular fibrillation that can cause sudden heart attacks. The Medicine candidates include Heartstream's lightweight defibrillators and the National Library of Medicine's digital library of human anatomy.

Non-competitive awards differ from competitive awards in several noteworthy ways. For starters, the candidates for non-competitive ("recognition") awards are "apples and oranges" rather than "likes."

Plus, there generally is a minimum winning requirement. Because candidates are individually measured against a standard of excellence, there is no guarantee that any of them will achieve the minimum winning requirement. Therefore, since all of the candidates may fall short of the prescribed mark, non-competitive awards are not must-give awards.[1]

An example of this type of award is the Deming Prize for Total Quality Management, given by the Japanese Union of Scientists and Engineers on an "as-deserved" basis. It may be given to one, more than one or no companies in any given year.

The hypothetical Good Egg Award and the actual Syd Cassyd Emmy Award also are non-competitive. They share a subjective element that does not occur in competitive awards.

Why does someone get the Good Egg? According to Mr. Widget, the award is given "from time to time to thank an employee who shows compassion and thoughtfulness."

Why does someone get the Syd Cassyd Award? According to the Emmy rules, for having "made a significant positive impact on the Academy through their efforts and service over many years of involvement."

Compare these subjective criteria with the flatly

---

[1] A variation on the non-compulsion to give an award is giving one at relatively long intervals. The Orville H. Gibson Guitar Awards were given to top guitarists only once every five years—until 1997, when they went on an annual cycle.

objective criterion of why a horse wins a race: "It is first across the finish line."

Because non-competitive awards do not have competitors, there is no opportunity to gain or give an advantage because of a competitor's error. If horses ran non-competitive races, they would run against a standard of excellence—e.g., a minimum time to run a length of track. If there were a field of horses attempting to "beat the clock" on the same track at the same time, a jockey turning his horse into the rail would give no advantage to any of the other horses, who are independently vying against nothing but the clock.

Like competitions, the outcome of non-competitive awards is never certain. Many of the same objective and subjective variables apply, and winning on one occasion does not guarantee it on the next.

Hybrid Awards

In general, competitive and non-competitive criteria are not linked in a single awards process, although they can be. Skating matches are an example of this conscious hybridization of the competitive and non-competitive. Each skater is judged on technical proficiency and dance performance.

The technical phase is designed to test the skaters' ability to do exactly the same fundamental moves on the ice. Because every skater is required to execute the same moves, the judges can objectively compare the technical ability of each skater in each separate execution. This is an "apples vs. apples" competition, and the skater who shows the greatest technical proficiency is "first across the line" with the highest cumulative score—clearly a competitive process.

The dance phase also requires the skaters to have technical proficiency, but here it becomes part of the background. The foreground is an interpretive, expressive and highly individualized performance. Each skater tries to strike a unique chord with the judges. Each has a different look, style and routine. Where they were all doing the same "apples" in the technical trials, here they are consciously striving for "apples and oranges." The judges must evaluate them according to a standard of excellence, rather than in competition with one another. This type of judging is a hallmark of non-competitive awards processes.

Another example of this hybrid awards process is a beauty pageant in which the contestants vie against one another in what is correctly known as the "swimsuit competition," but are judged individually when they showcase their talent with a vocal or instrumental performance, dramatic recitation, etc.

Hiring and college admissions often are other examples of the conscious hybridization of competitive and non-competitive processes. For instance, colleges may look first at only those applicants with the highest cluster of SAT scores (a "first across the line" competition), then factor in such non-competitive considerations as community service and indicators of personal maturity (adding "apples and oranges" to the equation). Or, in a hiring situation, employment chances may turn on competitive factors (the candidates' relative academic accomplishments) and non-competitive considerations (whether they are a "fit" for the culture of the company).

Once you've decided whether your awards program will be competitive or non-competitive—or a combination of the two—the next big question is: Who will be the judge of that?

Judges generally are chosen for their expertise in the achievements being considered for awards. Depending on the type of awards program your company is initiating, your clients may be the experts, your employees may be the experts, you may need to bring in an outside panel of experts, or you may prefer to make the final decision yourself.

The choice of judge (or judges) is bound to have a profound impact on the outcome of your awards program. Consider, for instance, two of your company's supervisors. Because they are different people, even when presented with the same list of criteria for an award, they may well select completely different winners. The more people you add to the mix, the more differences of opinion you'll get (a serious issue if a unanimous vote is required).

Also consider the differences between a critic's choice award and a people's choice award. Rarely do critics and the moviegoing public, for example, agree on their selections for Best Picture, Best Actor and so on.

When you are developing your awards program, you will need to determine whose opinion you consider most valuable. Also, bear in mind that the definition of *expertise* may vary. For instance, consider these awards and their judges:

- The Deming Prize awards committee is chaired by the head of the Japanese Union of Scientists and Engineers, with members drawn from academia, the officer ranks of firms that have implemented companywide quality control and other such experts—i.e., expertise based on business and educational experience.

- The Buckeye Children's Book Award, which is intended to encourage and enhance children's book reading, is nominated and voted on by school children—i.e., expertise based on their direct consumption of the product.

- The Golden Torch Award, given by the Insurance Marketing Communications Association for an outstanding contribution to property and casualty insurance communications, is voted on by a board of five insurance industry experts whose titles typically are "advertising manager" or "director of communications"—i.e., expertise based on professional experience.

- The Emmy for Lead Actor in a Drama Series is voted on by Television Academy members who are actors—i.e., expertise based on shared professional training and experience.

- On the other hand, the Oscar for Best Actor is voted on by all Motion Picture Academy members, including not only actors, but computer graphics designers, makeup artists, production designers, sound editors, etc.— i.e., expertise derived from a general savvy that comes with being a working professional in feature production.

- The Kenesaw M. Landis Award for the most valuable player in major league baseball is voted on by the Baseball Writers Association of America—i.e., expertise defined as a function of the journalists' observation, analysis, criticism and reportage of professional baseball players.

In the case of the Loebner Prize (a.k.a. the Turing Test Award), given by the Cambridge Center for Behavioral Studies, the usual concept of expertise is turned on its head. The Loebner judges are pitted against machines that try to emulate natural human behavior. Their challenge as judges is to determine whether responses on a computer terminal are being produced by a computer or by a person. Designers of the computer program that best succeeds in fooling the judges receive a cash award and a medal.

Narrow- and Broad-Based Electorates

Once you have identified the type of expertise you seek in your judge or judges, you will need to decide if your awards program will use a narrow- or broad- or mixed-based electorate. As you read through the following examples, identify which is most similar to and/or appropriate to your situation.

Here are a few examples of awards that are determined by a narrow-based electorate.

- The State Employment Security Agency National Awards winners are determined by a panel of seven judges composed of individuals not associated with the agency (commonly known as the Unemployment Office) and specifically designated according to type—i.e., a high-tech employer who actively goes through the office to hire workers; a representative from organized labor; an unemployed job seeker who was receiving unemployment insurance and actively using the agency's employment services to find a new job; an educator; etc.

- The Pulitzer Prizes are determined by a board of 19 members. In 1996, these included the president and journalism dean of Columbia University (which administers the awards), editors and publishers of large, medium and small-market newspapers, additional academics, a wire service (Associated Press) executive and one columnist (William Safire of the *New York Times*).

- The Television Academy's rules and procedures for the Syd Cassyd Founders Award require board ratification of a candidate proffered by the board's executive committee, which has 15 members.

- The Shanghai Television Festival's judging consists of 10 jurors who determine the nominees and another jury of 10 that determines the winners.

The following are examples of awards that are determined by a broad-based electorate.

- The Blockbuster Entertainment Awards are the largest publicly voted honors in the movie and music industries. In 1997, more than 11 million people cast their votes at in-store kiosks at more than 4,000 participating Blockbuster video and music stores, Planet Hollywood locations in North America and Japan, and via the Internet, making it the largest publicly voted awards show of any kind in the world. As an incentive to participate in the voting, Blockbuster offers the opportunity for voters to win trips to the awards presentation show.

- The Heisman Memorial Trophy for the outstanding college football player in the United States is voted on by more than 900 electors (TV and radio media, plus the prior Heisman winners).

- The Oscar for Best Picture is determined in a two-step process in which the full voting membership of the Academy of Motion Picture Arts & Sciences (AMPAS) casts the votes that determine the five nominees. Then, on a second round of voting, they cast the votes that determine the single winner.

- The American Music Awards derives its nominations from sales charts—e.g., the three best-selling rap records are the three nominations in the rap category. The nominations are then sent to a national sampling of approximately 20,000 people, who vote their preferences.

And the Winner Is ...

However, it is worth pointing out that there is not always a parallel between sales—or other measurable results—and awards. For instance, the 1996 Eclipse Award for the outstanding trainer in professional horse racing was given to Bill Mott, whose horses won six Grade I races and a total of $14 million. The runner-up was Wayne Lukas, whose horses won 13 Grade I races, including the Kentucky Derby and the Belmont Stakes, and earned a total of $15.9 million. Judging was done by turf writers, track secretaries and the *Daily Racing Form*, which also polled its readers. In the official vote, Mott won by a narrow margin of 123 to 112½ votes. *The Racing Form* poll gave Mott a 2 to 1 win over Lukas, with 1,600 to 810 votes.

A Two-Tier Voting Process

Most electorates lie between the extremes of the narrow- or broad-based examples noted above, often thanks to a two-tier voting process. Sometimes, a broad-based electorate nominates the candidates, then a narrow-based electorate casts the deciding votes. More often, however, the process works in the opposite direction.

Consider the following examples:

- The Oscar for Art Direction is determined in a two-step process, in which only the members of the AMPAS Art Direction Branch cast the votes that determine the three nominees. Then, on a second round of voting, the entire voting membership casts its votes to determine the single winner.

- The Screen Actors Guild Awards nominees are determined by balloting among 4,200 randomly selected guild members. The winners then are selected by the full voting membership of 86,000 SAG members.

- The Emmy for Movie of the Week is determined in a two-step process in which the full voting membership of the Academy casts the votes that determine the five nominees. Then, on a second round of voting, a group of 50 to 60 voters culled mainly from the Producer's Branch casts the votes that determine the single winner.

- The Malcolm Baldrige Award rules designate a Board of Examiners that "evaluates award applications, prepares feedback reports and makes award recommendations to the director of NIST. The board consists of business and quality experts primarily from the private sector. Members are selected by NIST through a competitive application process." The board consists of approximately 300 members, of which about 240 are examiners and 50 are senior examiners—but only 10 are judges.

- The short list of eligible candidates for the categories of the *Soap Opera Digest* Awards is determined by the magazine staff. The winners are then determined by those members of the public who effectively enfranchise themselves—by buying the issue of *Soap Opera Digest* containing the ballot, filling it out and sending it back to the magazine.

- The Victor Awards nominees are determined by the editors of *Sport Magazine*. The nominees then are voted on by the sports media throughout the country, with a single recipient chosen in each category.

- In a three-tier process, the Primetime Emmy Sound Mixing entries are voted on by the entire Sound Mixing Branch. The top 20 percent of the vote-getters are then advanced to a prenomination stage, in which tapes are screened by panels of sound mixing executives. The top five vote-getters that emerge from the screenings are the nominees, which are then screened by another panel of sound mixing executives, whose votes determine the winner.

- The Grammy for Album of the Year also is determined in a three-step process, in which the full 9,000-strong Academy membership votes for nominees. The top 20 vote-getters are reviewed by a 25-member secret panel, which determines which five will emerge as the nominees. A third round of voting by the full membership then determines the single winner.

Similarly, the CableAce cable television awards entries are screened by preliminary panels made up of all invited members of the Cable Academy. In the final judging, the panels are selected by the Cable Academy staff in conjunction with the National CableAce Competition Committee, and consist of professionals from various sectors of the programming industry.

The rules and procedures for competitions in which there are both nominees and winners also must note whether the judging will be a "double-pass" or "single-pass" system.

In a double-pass system, the accountants (or other trusted number-crunchers) tabulate both the nominees (top vote-getters) and the winner (*the* top vote-getter) from the same ballots. For example, if the rules call for three nominations, and Bob, Linda and Sally are the three top vote-getters, then they are announced as the nominees. When the accountants return to the ballots and find that Linda has more votes than Bob or Sally, then she is announced as the winner. The system is called a "double pass" because the first tabulation (or pass) of the ballots determines the nominees, and the second tabulation determines the winners.

A single-pass system would use the same procedure to determine the nominees, but the votes of a separate, subsequent panel would be used to determine the winners. The system is called a "single pass" because the accountants make a single tabulation (or pass) for each jury's ballots.

The advantage of a double-pass system is the convenience of not having to impanel another jury for the purpose of determining the winner, and having a consistent set of values brought to bear on both the entrants and the nominees. On the other hand, a single-pass system subjects the nominees to a fresh set of judges and a diversity of values. Because each has its practical and theoretical advantages, the Emmy Awards uses double pass in some competitions and single pass in others.

Judging Formats

Because of the differences between competitive and non-competitive awards, there are different judging formats appropriate to each.

Competitive awards require primarily quantitative judging formats—i.e., formats that roughly accomplish the same purpose as the stopwatches that time the relative speed of the competitors in the heat, or the cameras that verify the first horse across the finish line in a photo finish.

The simplest and most common quantitative judging format for competitive awards is the "top vote-getter" format—i.e., the candidate who gets more votes than the other competitors is the winner.

Another common quantitative format is a ratings system, in which one or more qualities are rated. The results may be totaled or averaged for the various categories.

The local chapters of the Emmy Awards use the following 1-10 ratings scheme:

- 1-2 = very poor;
- 3-4 = poor;
- 5-6 = fair;
- 7-8 = good; and
- 9-10 = very good.

The candidate with the highest cumulative score wins.

Similarly, the scoring system for the Baldrige awards is set up on an "ascending percentage" basis, in which 0 percent is the lowest score and 100 percent is the highest. A candidate's percentage score is based on how well it has fulfilled the performance expectations of the awards criteria. For example, how well has the company's education and training of employees served as a key vehicle in building the company's and employees' capabilities?

- If the score is 0 percent, the results are "poor."

- If the score is 10 percent to 30 percent, there are "good performance levels in a few areas."

- If the score is 40 percent to 60 percent, "good performance levels are reported for many to most areas of importance."

- If the score is 70 percent to 90 percent, "current performance is good to excellent in most areas of importance."

- If the score is 100 percent, "current performance is excellent" and can be characterized as "benchmark leadership" for the industry.

The American National Standards Institute uses a 1-4 scale. The ANSI awards have customized categories of evaluation for each of their five medals. The eligibility for the Astin-Polk International Standards Medal specifies it is for "promoting trade and understanding among nations through personal participation in the advancement, development or administration of international standardization, measurement or certification."

The judges consider the candidates according to their:

1) leadership accomplishments, which are rated on a 1-4 scale (4 being the best); and

2) contributions to the international standards community, which are rated on a 1-4 scale (4 being the best).

A third 1-4 rating based on other factors—their choice—is an option open to the Awards Committee.

Another type of quantitative format is "preferential voting," in which the candidates are ranked. For instance, the candidate preferred most by the voter gets a "1," the candidate liked second-best gets a "2," and so on, until a preference number has been assigned to all candidates. As with a golf score, the lowest preferential voting score wins.

Non-Competitive Judging Formats

Non-competitive judging formats are designed to individually measure each candidate against a standard of excellence, rather than against the other candidates.

The simplest and most common type of non-competitive judging is the "achievement of excellence" format—in which any candidate that receives a predesignated score or better is a winner. (Any of the above quantitative judging formats can be used to generate the scores.)

For instance, the 1995 Emmy judging panel ballot for Outstanding Achievement in Special Visual Effects required judges to vote yes (it should receive an Emmy) or no (it should not receive an Emmy) for each of the entrants. Any entry that received two-thirds of the total votes cast for it as "yes" won an Emmy. (A sample of the ballot appears in Appendix 1.)

A more general set of evaluation criteria in a non-competitive award situation is exemplified by the Corporation for Public Broadcasting Awards. Judges evaluate a broad range of entries—everything from radio documentaries to children's television programming—by means of the following six criteria:

1) Overall excellence;

2) Effectiveness of the program in communicating to and holding the attention of the audience;

3) Program concept and creative development of a theme and subject;

4) Authenticity of content;

5) Imaginative use of the production techniques and crafts specific to the medium; and

6) Use of talent.

Another option is to weight various categories according to their relative importance. An example of this is the non-competitive ratings-score system used by the Tournament of Roses Parade. Each float is judged on its own merits. However, the Fantasy & Imagination and Most Spectacular Float categories are "face value" scores—they are recorded at their actual value. The Design and Concept score is weighted by a factor of three—i.e., a score of 5 becomes a 15. And because the Rose Parade primarily emphasizes floral displays, the Use and Presentation of Flowers category is weighted by a factor of six—so a 5 becomes a 30—the heaviest weight carried by any category of evaluation.

Juried Awards

Yet another option when it comes to judging is using an awards jury. It works much like a courtroom jury: The awards jury both witnesses and deliberates on the evidence presented, and can benefit from a give and take in a search for consensus. Juried voting, with its emphasis on open discussion, could be considered the opposite of a secret ballot.

Broad-based electorates are logistically precluded from juried voting. But, for some narrow-based electorates, juried voting can be useful for developing a more informed electorate.

Again, you may wish to develop a hybrid system. For example, the Tournament of Roses Parade uses a multistage judging process that combines ballots and juried voting.

The 1997 Rose Parade had 57 floats competing for 22 Banner Trophies, including the Humor Award for "most comical and amusing entry," the Theme Award for "excellence in presenting the parade theme in design and flowers" and the Governor's Award for "best depiction of life in California."

As noted above, the judges used a weighted-ratings system. They would record their numerical ratings (from 1 to 10) for 14 separate float characteristics (Creative Design and Concept, Depiction of U.S.A. Life, etc.).

The ratings-score system was used to non-competitively evaluate each float—i.e., each of the three judges considered the individual merit of each float and rated it without comparing it to the other floats. This was done for the first time on December 30 (with the floats in a preliminary state of preparation) and repeated on

December 31 (when the floats were more or less completed and ready for the parade).

At the conclusion of the second tour of the floats, the judges retired to a closed session and determined the winner of each Banner Award. It was during this New Year's Eve parley that the judging switched from a non-competitive evaluation of each float on its own terms to the head-to-head competition among the finalists in each category of competition—a process that would ultimately produce the winners.

Dr. James Loper, who served as one of the judges, said, "We began by agreeing on the best candidates for each award, then positioned and repositioned them until we reached consensus on a winner in each. The ratings scores were very useful as reminders of how we had evaluated the floats earlier that day and the day before, and they gave us guidance when we came to impasses that might otherwise have left us with ties.

"In effect, we began the process by individually evaluating the overall merit of each float, and we concluded it by eliminating all but the best in each category."

A similar juried system is used by the San Francisco International Film Festival, but juries reserve the right to grant one, more than one or no awards per category.

An example of a narrow-based juried award in the Primetime Emmys is the Engineering Award. (The Engineering Award will serve as a recurring example, because it is a useful paradigm for many association, charity and company awards.) A committee chair is appointed by the Academy president, and committee members are recruited by the chair. Their charge, according to the rules, is to consider all engineering developments that have proven their efficacy during the awards year—and to determine which, if any, merit an Engineering Emmy Award or Engineering Plaque.

The first committee meeting—generally in early May—is held after the annual rollout of the latest technical products at the National Association of Broadcasters convention. Between the entries and items brought to the committee for consideration by its members, approximately 20 to 30 candidates are up for consideration. These are subdivided into three groups: 1) out of contention; 2) tabled to next year because they are new and their industry acceptance and efficacy has not yet been shown; and 3) in contention for either an Engineering Plaque or Engineering Emmy.

Each item in contention is then assigned to a committee member for further investigation.

At the second meeting, the report on each candidate is given and discussed, and a vote is taken to decide: 1) now out of contention; 2) now in contention for an Engineering Plaque; or 3) now in contention for an Engineering Emmy.

Candidates that receive a unanimous "Yes" vote on any of the three counts are forwarded to the Board of Governors for ratification at the next board meeting, where they are introduced by the chairman of the committee, discussed and either ratified as Engineering Plaque or Engineering Emmy winners or removed from contention (tabled to next year or dismissed entirely).

Candidates that remain in contention but require further investigation are tabled to a third meeting, where the above process is repeated—possibly even into a fourth meeting—until all candidates are voted out of contention, tabled until next year, or ratified for a plaque or an Emmy.

The jury process that produces the engineering awards is appropriate to the difficulty inherent in the mission, the complexity of the technical hardware and software that must be reviewed, and the fact that it is engaged—as juries often are—in both a competitive and non-competitive judging process. In this case, it is competitive because it considers candidates that do similar tasks (e.g., digital editing systems) and must decide which is superior. It continues in the competitive mode by determining if the superior candidate is as good as existing technology and, if it is, if it is merely derivative of that technology or a real engineering breakthrough. If the answer is affirmative, the jury must then switch over to a non-competitive mode and apply the Achievement of Excellence test (noted above) to determine if it is plaque- or Emmy-worthy.

The jury process is, in large part, repeated when the recommendations are presented to the Board of Governors. Arguments pro and con are presented in both the competitive and non-competitive areas of consideration. Additionally, the board—as can happen with any board for a company, charity or association—may well introduce political criteria that supersede engineering achievement (e.g., colorization of black and white movies may be a brilliant engineering feat, but directors and cinematographers condemn it as an inappropriate revision of the auteur's original and will lobby their fellow board members to dismiss it as heretical technology).

To summarize key points about the judging process:

- Is there an ideal number of judges? Emmy rules require at least 12 per panel—the logic being that if 12 jurors can hang a man, then the same number ought to be able to choose a winner.

- Whatever their number, judges must be competent to evaluate the candidates according to the rules of the competition. If the judges' expertise is not trusted by those who give and receive the award, get new judges.

- Going directly from entries to winners is the tidiest kind of competition, but it deprives all parties involved of the anticipation that comes with having nominations. Competitions without nominations are tributes. With nominations, they are dramas.

- The best judging system is the one that contributes to the perceived value of the award. Knowing that there are no two top awards that use exactly the same judging process should encourage you to creatively shape your system to fulfill your award's mission.

Procedures for Entries and Nominees

Once you have determined who will be eligible to win—as well as who will be eligible to nominate and vote for candidates—the next big decision is how to handle the mechanics of the voting process.

This includes creating, sending out and counting ballots, determining how to deal with ties, verifying the information on ballots and more.

These issues also will need to be clarified by the awards program's rules and procedures.

In this chapter, we will begin at the beginning of the awards process—from the entrants' point of view. We'll start with the call for entries.

The Entry Form

Non-competitive, or recognition, awards given by a company, charity or association may or may not require entry forms. However, competitive awards generally require some kind of entry form—or additional entry material—that can be used by the judges to evaluate the achievement.

If you are going to require entry forms for your awards program, you will need to determine what information is required for judging, including any additional material that must be submitted for evaluation purposes. You also will need to provide some information for the candidates—such as what would be needed to determine eligibility and to select the categories in which they will enter.

A succinct entry form is not always possible, but certainly preferable to a dauntingly long and complex one. As Montaigne suggested in his essay *Of Recompenses of Honour* (Essays 11, 7), "The rules for dispensing this new order had need to be extremely clipt and bound under great restrictions, to give it authority."

User-friendly entry forms do not try the time and patience of the entrant. They gather and dispense only that information essential to placing the entrant in the competition. In effect, they are selectively edited versions of the awards rules, procedures, calendar and budget that have at their core an abbreviated explanation of or a reference to:

- what the awards are (rules);

- how the process of choosing winners is to be implemented (procedures);

- when the various stages of the process will occur (calendar), and

- what (if anything) the entrant will have to pay in order to compete (budget).

Some awards entry forms are supplemented by commentaries that analyze "what the judges want." For example, as we mentioned in Chapter 6, the *Ad & PR Awards Competition Alert* is a monthly publication about "opportunities to win recognition as the best in advertising, public relations, marketing and communications." Not only does it provide readers with information about eligibility, categories, deadlines, judging and entry procedures, fees and contacts, but it also advises them on strategy.

For instance, the *Alert* points out that the prestigious Silver Anvil Award requires a "concise, two-page summary addressing each of the four criteria (research, planning, execution and evaluation) for a PR program that has 'successfully addressed a contemporary issue with exemplary skill and resourcefulness.' " The commentary advises that the "two-page summary of your program is the single most important part of your entry. Judges will look at it first to decide if your entry is worthy of further consideration."

Also, the *Alert* says, "Make sure you pick the right category for your entry. Judges cannot transfer entries to other categories and will eliminate those submitted in an incorrect category." And a final tip: "You stand a better chance of winning if your program is near completion, when evaluation against initial objectives can be better determined."

Clearly, the *Alert*'s advice holds true for many awards competitions, and you may wish to include similar tips and reminders at the top of your entry form.

The 1996 entry form for the Primetime Emmy Awards, which appears in Appendix 2, selectively edits the competition's 62-page rules book (which details all aspects of the competition) down to two sides of an 8.5x11-inch sheet of paper.

The form's purpose is twofold:

1) to get "incoming" information necessary for the Academy to place the entrant in the competition; and

2) to give the entrant enough "outgoing" information about the competition rules, procedures, calendar and budget to make the entry.

The incoming information serves to identify the entrant (name, address, phone and fax numbers). It also identifies the entrant's achievement by requiring the entrant to:

- choose a category of competition (there are more than 70 separate categories in the Primetime Awards);
- state the program title;
- state the network;
- state the original air date;
- state the running time;
- state the production company; and
- provide any special information relevant to certain categories—e.g., a synopsis of the program or the name of the actor-entrant's character.

The outgoing information serves to:

- notify the entrant of eligibility dates;
- notify the entrant of special rules;
- notify the entrant of the entry fee structure; and
- notify the entrant of the procedure for confirming receipt of the entry.

And remember, all this is done on one double-sided piece of paper.

(Another sample entry form, for the 1995-96 Emmy for Outstanding Achievement in Engineering Development, appears in Appendix 3.)

Sometimes, entrants will be able to fill in the blanks on your form and consider themselves entered. Sometimes, they will need to work a bit harder.

For example, the Pulitzer Prizes for journalism require entrants to provide an exhibit, in scrapbook form, of news stories, editorials, photographs or cartoons as published, with the name of the paper and the date of publication.

In addition, the entry form stipulates that:

- Up to three individuals may be named on a team entry; otherwise, the entry must be made in the name of the staff of the newspaper.

- Any significant challenge to the accuracy or fairness of an entry, such as published letters, corrections, retractions, as well as responses by the newspaper, should be included in the submission.

- In the photography categories, no entry whose content is manipulated or altered, apart from standard newspaper cropping and editing, will be deemed acceptable.

- Exhibits must be presented in scrapbooks measuring no more than 12x17 inches, except in cases where a full newspaper page is required to make clear the full scope and impact of the material entered.

- All exhibits should include biographies and pictures of entrants and each entry must be accompanied by a handling fee of $50 made payable to Columbia University/Pulitzer Prizes.

The Baldrige Award entry form, although lengthy, also satisfies the basic requirements for an entry form—and it makes entrants to the competition do their homework. Its principal information-gathering section is divided into seven parts that ask the applying company about leadership, information and analysis, strategic planning, human resource development and management, process management, business results, and customer focus and satisfaction.

Here is an abbreviated survey of the seven categories and the information required of the entrant:

1) The leadership section "addresses how the company's senior executives set strategic directions and build and maintain a leadership system conducive to high performance, individual development and organizational learning." The applicant needs to explain:

    a. how senior executives provide effective leadership and direction in building and improving company competitiveness, performance and capabilities ...

    b. how senior executives evaluate and improve the effectiveness of the company's leadership system and organization to pursue performance excellence goals ...

2) The information and analysis category "examines the management and effectiveness of the use of data and information to support customer-driven performance excellence and marketplace success." The applicant is asked to explain:

    a. how information and data needed to drive improvement of overall company performance are selected and managed ...

    b. how the company evaluates and improves the selection, analysis and integration of information and data, aligning them with the company's business priorities ...

3) Strategic planning "examines how the company sets strategic directions, and how it determines key plan requirements. Also examined is how the plan requirements are translated into an effective performance management system." The applicant is asked to report:

    a. how the company develops strategies and business plans to strengthen its customer-related, operational and financial performance and its competitive position ...

    b. how strategies and plans are translated into actionable key business drivers, which serve as the basis for deploying plan requirements ...

4) Human resources development and management examines "how the work force is enabled to develop and utilize its full potential, aligned with the company's performance objectives." How does the company:

    a. translate its overall requirements from strategic and business planning to specific resource plans?

    b. evaluate and improve its human resource planning and practices and the alignment of the plans and practices with the company's strategic and business directions?

5) Process management "examines the key aspects of process management, including customer-focused design, product and service delivery processes, support services and supply management involving all work units, including research and development. The category examines how key processes are designed, effectively managed and improved to achieve higher performance." It is the area of the entry that addresses:

    a. how products, services and production/ delivery processes are designed ...

    b. how product, service and production/ delivery process designs are reviewed and/or tested in detail to ensure trouble-free launch ...

    c. how designs and design processes are evaluated and improved so that introductions of new or modified products and services progressively improve in quality and cycle time ...

6) Business results "examines the company's performance and improvement in key business areas—product and service quality, productivity and operational effectiveness, supply quality and financial performance indicators linked to these areas." The applicant is asked to provide:

   a. current levels and trends in key measures and/or indicators of product and service quality. [Graphs and tables are encouraged.]

   b. how the company addresses future requirements and expectations of customers ...

7) Customer focus and satisfaction "examines the company's systems for customer learning and for building and maintaining customer relationships." In this final evaluation category, the applicant explains:

   a. how the company determines current and near-term requirements and expectations of customers ...

   b. how the company addresses future requirements and expectations of customers ...

   c. how the company evaluates and improves its processes for determining customer requirements and expectations ...

If the entry form for the highly respected Baldrige Awards proves anything, it's that you shouldn't hesitate to ask for the information you need to make a truly informed, fair and accurate judgment. However, be aware that—in general—the more information you ask for, the fewer entries you are likely to receive.

Asking Entrants to Rate Themselves

The AT&T/University of Rhode Island Quality in Education application form follows the same pattern as the Baldrige Awards form. But, after gathering basic information about the entrant (school name, address, name of principal, private or public school, size of the school and school system, etc.), it formalizes and simplifies inquiries about leadership, information and analysis, organizational planning, human resources and management, quality assurance of programs and services, quality results and constituent satisfaction by repeatedly asking the same seven questions.

For example, under Category I—Leadership, it says:

1) Senior Administrators

Are all senior administrators personally involved in the process of developing and maintaining an environment focused on excellence? Are they visibly involved in quality-related activities, such as goal setting, long- and short-term planning, reviewing student performance, communicating with teachers, students, parents and other constituents, and recognizing the contributions that teachers, administrators, and service and support staff make as individuals and as groups?

1. To what extent does your school/school system fulfill the criteria:

    ☐ Yes, completely   ☐ Mostly
    ☐ Somewhat Rarely   ☐ Not at all

2. Describe the process your school/school system uses.

3. Describe and demonstrate the extent to which this criteria is being satisfied.

4. Rate the importance of this element to your organization:

    (Significantly) 5   4   3   2   1 (Not at all)

5. To what extent has this process been improved over the last three years?

    (A great deal) 5   4   3   2   1 (Not at all)

6. Rate your continuous improvement priority:

    (High priority) 5   4   3   2   1 (Low priority)

7. What are your planned improvement actions?

2) Organizational and Quality Values

Does your school/school system have clearly articulated quality values that are projected in a consistent manner, adopted throughout the school/school system and continuously reinforced? Do written policy, mission and vision statements, long- and short-term plans, and other operational guidelines reflect and support quality values as they have been articulated?

Then the form repeats the above seven questions, as it does under each category for the rest of the entry form.

Grant Applications

Entry forms for association awards that consist of money are typically known as grant applications. But like any competitive award entry form, they contain the standard elements noted above.

For example, the application for the American Gastroenterological Association's $50,000 award for gastric cancer research is divided into seven sections:

1) A description of the award, the association's objectives, eligibility, the award and the requirements placed on the investigator, the selection criteria, the review process and the deadline for entries.

2) Instructions for filling out the form.

3) General information about the applicant.

4) An abstract of the proposed research.

5) Signature of the applicant and research sponsor—e.g., the applicant's division or department head.

6) A summary checklist of all the application requirements in sections 2 through 5 above.

7) Optional personal data (sex, race/ethnic origin, age).

Crafting a Sample Entry Form

As an example of how you might draft an entry form for your awards competition, consider the hypothetical Widget Co.'s Widgie Awards—a competition for design improvements in Widgets. Its user-friendly entry form might be as follows:

The 5th Annual Widgie Awards for
Design Improvement in Widgets

Official Entry Form

All entries must be submitted to the office of the president of the Widget Co. by 5 p.m., December 31, 1996. An entry fee of $50 must accompany this form. The board will review the entries and, if necessary, request additional information. Nomination(s) (one, more than one or none) will be announced on March 1, 1997. Award(s) (one, more than one or none) in the form of a Widgie statuette and $5,000 will be presented to each winner at the Widget Co.'s annual meeting at the Ritz-Carlton Huntington Hotel in Pasadena, California, on June 15, 1997.

Name, address, phone and fax number of entrant(s).

Has this improvement been entered in this competition before? _ Yes   _ No

If so, in what year?

Expected status of improvement on December 31, 1996 (check one):

__ on the drawing board

__ in a prototype stage

__ ready for on-line implementation

Is there a patent or patent pending on this improvement? _ Yes   _ No

What is the area of improvement (check one or more)?

__ Widget mechanicals

__ Widget electronics

__ Widget opticals

Describe the improvement in 50 words or less.

Describe what makes the improvement "Widgie Award"-worthy in 50 words or less.

Entrant's signature/date.

This entry form places the entrant in the competition without subjecting his or her submission to a definitive examination of its Widgie Award-worthiness. The judging process may require additional information from the entrant, but that is a separate stage of the awards process.

Although entry forms are usually a means of tossing one's own hat into the ring, they can be limited to the entry of someone else. The American National Standards Institute's entry form is headed "Nominating a Colleague." It allows a "third party" to recommend either an individual or a company for any or all of the five ANSI medals.

Making Entry Forms Available

The distribution of entry forms is the formal call for entries into the competition. For big, high-dollar awards competitions, the entry form could be made available to all potential entrants by means of an exhaustive mail, public relations and advertising campaign.

For instance, the Academy distributes Primetime

entry forms by mail to members of the Academy, networks, studios, production companies, industry guilds and unions, and talent agencies. It also sends out press releases to the industry trade papers (*Daily Variety*, *Hollywood Reporter*, etc.) and takes out ads in the industry trade papers and the Academy's *Emmy Magazine* announcing the startup of the competition.

You probably will want to follow suit for any external awards program. For starters, you would issue a press release announcing the startup of the competition—and work to have it published in your industry's trade magazines, newsletters and newspapers, as well as any guild or union newsletters, internal network communications, etc. A typical press release would simply alert potential entrants to the basic concept of the awards competition, as well as the deadline for entries.

Depending on the type of awards program, you also might want to take out an ad in the relevant publications to publicize the call for entries—or even arrange to run a copy of the entry form in a magazine or one of your industry associations' newsletters.

Careful records should be kept of the entry form distribution, as a defensive measure against the inevitable complaints from would-be entrants who missed the deadline. "I never got an entry form!" and "Why wasn't I notified the competition was underway?" are often heard at the Academy. They would be legitimate complaints about the conduct of the competition, were they not refuted with mailing house records, press notices and advertisements detailing the distribution of entries and the startup of the competition.

Receipt Confirmation

The logistics of acknowledging the receipt of entries can be mind-boggling (and cost-prohibitive for some companies or associations). However, the importance of a formal means of confirming receipt of entries can be illustrated by an incident that occurred during the 1980 Primetime Emmys:

When the Performer Ballot was issued, Frank Konigsberg, executive producer of the CBS miniseries *Guyana Tragedy: The Story of Jim Jones*, called the Academy to ask why the Lead Actor entry for Powers Boothe was omitted from the ballot. The answer was that no entry had been received, and only those who entered the competition appeared on the ballot.

Konigsberg insisted that he had made the entry on behalf of Boothe.

The Academy reiterated that it did not have possession of the entry form.

The argument went back and forth until Konigsberg signed a legal affidavit attesting to his delivery of the entry form, and Boothe was added to a supplementary ballot. (He then went on to win the Emmy at a telecast that was boycotted by every other on-strike member of the Screen Actors Guild—except Boothe, who surprised everyone by showing up and accepting his Emmy!)

The next year, the Academy instituted a new policy of issuing receipts for entries. The policy is noted on the back page of the entry form:

A faxed copy of the front page of this entry, stamped with the date that ATAS received it, will be your receipt that the entry was received by the Academy. If you do not receive the faxed receipt within 10 days of submitting the entry form, call the Academy.

Subsequently, when people call to complain that they had entered and were left off the ballot, they are asked to produce their entry receipts. Most cannot, but those who can are placed on a supplementary ballot and entered into the competition.

Another example of entry confusion occurred in the 1996 Grammy Awards. Songwriter Jim Steinman thought his single *It's All Coming Back to Me Now* (on Celine Dion's *Falling Into You* album) would be entered by Sony Music, the album's record company. According to the *Los Angeles Times*, Sony did enter the song in a number of categories, but not the one that would have put Steinman into eligibility to win a songwriting Grammy.

Steinman's manager said, "He was told the song was left off for fear that it possibly would cancel out another Dion hit, *Because You Loved Me*, written by Diane Warren" and appearing on the same album.

As a result, *It's All Coming Back to Me Now*—which ranked among the most-played songs on radio in 1996 and which catapulted the Dion album to the national No. 1 spot that summer—was not among the 511 best song entries.

Similarly, *Home Improvement* star Tim Allen was left off the ballots for Emmy Award consideration in 1994, and the much-lauded basketball documentary *Hoop Dreams* failed to receive an Academy Award nomination in 1995. But Allen's omission was due to a simple filing error by his show's staff, and *Hoop*

Who's Doing the Entering?

Dreams was left out due to a nominating committee's judgment—not deliberate decisions based on record company politics and marketing strategies.

"It's wrong to put this in the hands of a record company and let politics take over," said Steinman's agent.

Why didn't Steinman just nominate himself—or get another Academy member to nominate him? Any Academy member can submit a song or artist for consideration, but in practice it largely has been left to the record companies. Steinman's agent, in fact, is a member—but he says that based on past experience, he had no reason to believe his client's song would not be submitted by Sony, and was unaware that it hadn't been until the deadline had passed.

The incontrovertible lesson of the unfortunate omissions of both Tim Allen (Emmys) and Jim Steinman (Grammys) is: If you want to make sure your entry gets on the ballot, enter it yourself!

Processing Completed Forms

As important as it is to establish a defensible position with regard to the distribution of entry forms, the same caution should apply to the acceptance of entry forms. Outbound or inbound, entry forms must be monitored very carefully. They are the key to the integrity of the initial phase of the competition.

Most Primetime Emmy Awards entries are incorrect or incomplete. If they are not corrected, they can cause significant problems in the subsequent phases of the competition. An example is the error that resulted in Dennis Miller losing a nomination in the 1995 competition:

Chapter 11—Procedures for Entries and Nominees

Dennis Miller Live! on HBO was entered in the 1995 Primetime Emmy Awards in Category 62—Variety, Music or Comedy Series. This is the category that mainly pits late-night talk shows, such as *The Tonight Show Starring Jay Leno* and *Late Night With David Letterman* against one another.

If *Dennis Miller Live!* went on to win, Emmys would be awarded to the producers and, as the rules state, to the "host if his/her name is in the program title." Since Dennis Miller's name was in the program title, he would win an award as host if the series won.

Because Dennis Miller had mandatory eligibility with the team of producers in Category 62, he could not make another entry in Category 54, which is for hosts/performers in variety, music or comedy programs. The reason he could not make the additional entry goes back to a basic tenet of the Emmys (and most awards): A person is limited to one Emmy per achievement. If he were allowed to enter as host of *Dennis Miller Live!* in Category 62 (programs competing against programs) and again in Category 54 (individuals competing against individuals), he could potentially win two Emmys for the single achievement of being host of his show.

But an incorrect entry was made for Dennis Miller in Category 54. It should have been corrected—that is, thrown out of eligibility—before it was placed on the Performer Ballot. Unfortunately, the error was not caught until after Dennis Miller was announced as one of the nominees in Category 54. At that point, a representative from *Politically Incorrect With Bill Maher* called to ask why Bill Maher—whose eligibility in both Category 62 and 54 was parallel to Dennis Miller's eligibility in those two categories—had been denied entry in Category 54 and Dennis Miller had not. The Academy's response was that an error had been made and would be corrected at once.

Regrettably, there was no recourse but to disqualify the nomination. Per a Primetime rule, ineligible entries must be disqualified at any stage of the competition—even after they had emerged from the pack as nominations. Mr. Miller followed up with a gracious press release to the effect that mistakes will happen and that Barbara Streisand, who was also nominated in the category (and a favorite for the Emmy that she ultimately won) "could now get some sleep."

The Steps the Emmys Follow

Once the entries are received, the Academy begins to take the five steps involved in processing entries:

Step 1: Database Conversion

Step 2: Proofing for Common Errors

Step 3: Proofing for "Special Rules" Errors

Step 4: Ballot Preparation

Step 5: Press Release Preparation

The first step is inputting the information on the entry form into a computerized database file, which allows for a ready and convenient means of manipulating the data. You can print out labels based on this information, tally entries in a given category and perform any number of other functions based on the fields set up in the database.

After the information has been entered, it's time to begin proofing. This process is designed to stave off

Chapter 11—Procedures for Entries and Nominees

possible problems, including the possibility of an individual winning two awards for a single achievement—and the possibility of an individual not winning enough votes to be nominated simply because the person's (or the program's) name was spelled two different ways, splitting the votes and precluding a nomination.

The following are a few of the proofing procedures used at the Emmys.

The purpose of this proof is to detect and correct erroneous variations in program titles. The computer is programmed to list in alphabetical order the titles of all programs represented by all entries in the competition. If *The Third Annual Pablo Casals Festival* is entered two times—for the program entry in the Cultural Music/Dance category and the sound mixing entry in the Sound Mixing for a variety or music program—the computer would correctly show it as:

The Third Annual Pablo Casals Festival

The Third Annual Pablo Casals Festival

If the person making the sound mixing entry listed the title incorrectly as *3rd Annual Pablo Casals Festival,* the entries would not "stack." Rather, the correct entry would be alphabetized under "Third" in the T's, and the incorrect entry would precede the A-Z list, since Arabic numbers cannot be alphabetized and are programmed to appear prior to the alphabetical list.

If the error were not detected and corrected and both entries were nominated, the statistical summary would incorrectly list one nomination for *The Third Annual ...* and one nomination for *3rd Annual ...—*

Program Title
Proof

rather than two nominations for *The Third Annual* ...

The error would be caught, however, because it is standard proofing procedure to try to find an A-Z "home" for program titles beginning with Arabic numbers. The proofer would check under "Third" in the T's and find the *The Third Annual Pablo Casals Festival*. He or she then would note that it was a program entry, which can only be made by the program's producer. Since the producer has the final say on all credits for the program—including the form of the title—the proofer would know that *The Third Annual* ... is the correct title for the entry.

Another advantage of the A-Z "stacks" is their visual repetition, which makes it easy to find title variations. For example, if *NYPD Blue* were entered 10 times, the variations would stand out, as with *N.Y.P.D.*

Multiple Entry Proof for Programs

The purpose of this proof is to detect and correct a program or series being entered in more than one program category. For instance, *The Yearling*, a TV movie where *Little House on the Prairie* meets *Bambi*, could be entered in either the Movie of the Week or Children's Special categories, but not in both. If it were allowed to compete in two categories, it could win two Emmys—which, once again, would contradict the rule that a single achievement is limited to a single award.

To accomplish this proof, the computer is programmed to list in alphabetical order the titles of all programs represented by all entries in the competition in one column, then list the categories in which the entries were made in a second column. For instance:

Chapter 11—Procedures for Entries and Nominees

The Yearling   Movie of the Week

The Yearling   Children's Program

The proofer would note the illegal multiple entry in two program categories and contact the entrants—more than likely, two producers who each made a separate entry without consulting one another on the category placement. They would then be able to choose to enter the program in either the Movie of the Week or the Children's Program category. (If they could not decide or were unavailable to make the decision, the Awards Committee would determine the placement of the program.)

This is a variation on the above proof for programs. It uses a computer listing of individual entrants (in alphabetical order) in the first column, program titles in the second column and the category in which they are entered in the third column:

Jones, Bob	*ER*	Directing—Drama Series
Jones, Bob	*NYPD Blue*	Directing—Drama Series

Multiple Entry Proof for Individuals

It is a rule of the competition that individuals cannot enter more than once in the same category. The proofer would pull the entry cards and see who made the entries. If Mr. Jones made both entries, he would be asked to choose one or the other. If he made one and a producer made one on his behalf, the Academy would automatically take his.

If both entries were made by producers on his behalf, he would be asked if he wanted to make a choice.

If he did not want to make a choice—probably because he worked for both producers and did not want to offend either one—the producers would be asked if one would withdraw in favor of the other's entry. If neither would withdraw, the entry with the earliest receipt date would be chosen. If they both had the same receipt date, *ER* would be chosen, because *ER* precedes *NYPD Blue* in the alphabet.

These are just the sort of what-to-do-if scenarios that need to be clarified in advance in your awards program's rules and procedures.

Inconsistent Categorization Proof

The purpose of this proof is to detect and correct inconsistencies in the placement of entries. A general rule for the placement of individual achievement entries (e.g., performer or writer entries) is that they must follow the lead of the program entry.

When *Moonlighting* (with Bruce Willis and Cybill Shepherd) was entered by the producers as a drama series, Mr. Willis and Ms. Shepherd were compelled to enter their respective drama series performance categories. Had the producers of this "Dramedy" (i.e., a program comprised of roughly equal parts of comedy and drama) entered the program as a comedy series, Mr. Willis and Ms. Shepherd would have followed suit and entered in their respective comedy series performance categories. (In fact, the producers of *Moonlighting* entered the program as a comedy series in 1985 and the following year as a drama series.)

To facilitate the proof, the computer prints a three-column listing of the program title, the individual and the program category. The proofer notes the placement of the program as entered by the producers (which the computer always places at the top of the list), then scans the other categories for inconsistencies. In the following hypothetical stack, Mr. Willis's entry is incorrect and Ms. Shepherd's entry is correct:

Moonlighting [names of producers]Drama Series

Moonlighting Cybill Shepherd Lead Actress
Drama Series

Moonlighting Bruce Willis Lead Actor
Comedy Series

This proof is used to determine whether the correct network has been assigned to an entry. Visual repetition in stacks of program titles and networks is the key to an easy and accurate proofing process.

Note how apparent the "CBS" error is in this stack of entries for the medical drama *ER*, broadcast on NBC:

ER	NBC
ER	NBC
ER	NBC
ER	NBC
ER	CBS
ER	NBC
ER	NBC

Network Proof

This is a variation on the network proof. Note how inconsistencies in the righthand margin direct the proofer to the two errors in this stack for *Seinfeld*,

**Production
Company Proof**

which is produced by Castle Rock Entertainment Co.:

Seinfeld	Castle Rock Entertainment Co.
Seinfeld	Castle Rock Entertainment Co.
Seinfeld	Castle Rok Entertainment Co.
Seinfeld	Castle Rock Entertainment Co.
Seinfeld	Castle Rock Entertainment Co.
Seinfeld	Castle Rock
Seinfeld	Castle Rock Entertainment Co.

Proofing for "Special Rules" Errors

Once the entries have been proofed for common errors (typos, misspellings, errors on entry forms), Step 3 is to proof for "special rules" errors.

The Dennis Miller error described at the beginning of this chapter was the result of an oversight during the proofing for special rules errors. In the Dennis Miller case, the special rule was that hosts of variety, music and comedy programs who have their names in their programs' titles must enter and have sole eligibility in the program vs. program competition. They are precluded by a special rule from entering as hosts in the variety/music performer vs. variety/music performer competition.

Obviously, special rule proofing requires knowledge of the special rules and the categories of the competition to which they refer. Here are additional examples of special rules and the appropriate instructions for the proofers.

Category 2: Art Direction for a Series

Special Rule: Entrants for a series that had eligibility in a prior awards year must submit a videotape along with their entry form of the episode that, if nominated, they plan to submit to the judging panel that will determine the winner in this category. Two-thirds of the sets or locales used in the episode must be new to the series in this awards year.

The purpose of this rule is to make sure that this year's Emmy-winning achievements mainly first appeared on current series episodes and were not just carry-overs from a prior year.

Implementation of the special rule:

- Print a list of all entries in this category.

- Cross out those that are new this year. (We know their sets and locales are new to this year's competition.)

- Make sure that the entries remaining on the list are accompanied by a tape. If there is no tape, call the entrant and arrange for a tape to be sent to you.

- Notify the governors for the Art Directors Branch when the tapes are ready for review. The governors are responsible for setting up a panel to review them. Their review must be completed by May 15.

- After the tapes have been reviewed, the governors will notify you if any entries are ineligible. Call up the ineligibles and tell them what happened and why they are ineligible. If they wish to appeal, notify the governors, who will follow up with them.

- Revise the computer list of eligible entries as needed. Code the ineligible entries as "I." In the notes box, write "Not two-thirds new sets and locales." Then note your initials and the date.

- Return the tapes and entry fees of ineligibles. Enclose a refund request form so that the ineligibles will have written confirmation that the entry has been disqualified.

Category 10: Costuming for a Series

Special Rule: If there is a costume designer on the credits for a series, costumers who are also credited on the series are not eligible. Note that if a costume designer is designated as doing only the costumes for one of the stars of the series, the special rule is waived and costumers may enter alongside the costume designer for the star.

If there is a costume designer on a series, he/she designs most of the clothes worn by the stars. He/she is responsible for the "look" of the show's wardrobe. If there is also a costumer on the series, he/she takes a secondary role to the designer and mainly serves as a wardrobe supervisor for the extras. Because the Emmy is reserved for the principal creator of the look of the show's wardrobe, only the costume designer is eligible.

If the costume designer is designated in the credits as solely assigned to one of the stars, then the costumer has much more responsibility for the overall look of the show's wardrobe and may enter alongside the costume designer for the star. In effect, the costume designer for the star and costumer for the rest of the cast work as a team of principal creators and should rightly share credit for an Emmy-winning achievement.

Special rule implementation:

- Print an alphabetical list of the programs entered in Category 12—Costume Design for a Series.

- Print an alphabetical list of the programs entered in Category 10—Costuming for a Series.

- Check to see if the same program appears on both lists. If it does, check the costume designer's credit. If he/she is not designated as solely assigned to a star, disqualify the costumer. If he/she is designated as solely assigned to a star, leave both entries in the competition.

- If costumers are disqualified, revise the computer list of eligible entries as needed. Code the ineligible entries as "I." In the notes box, write "Costume Designer on series." Then note your initials and the date.

- Notify the ineligibles. If they worked on another series where there was no costume designer that would disqualify them, give them the opportunity to make another entry for that series. If not, refund their entry fees. Enclose a refund request form so that the ineligibles will have written confirmation that the entry has been disqualified.

Category 70: Sound Editing for a Series

Special rule: Only one entry per series per sound house or studio.

The supervising sound editor and his or her team of editors are asked to select their best episode and submit it as representative of the work they did throughout the season on the series. If the sound editing for the series was subbed out to more than one sound house or studio, then the separate teams from each sound house or studio may each choose an episode that represents their best work and submit it for Emmy consideration.

Special rule implementation:

- Print out a list of program titles for Category 70—Sound Editing for a Series. In the second column of the printout, have the computer list the sound house or studio at which the episode was sound edited.

- If you see the same series listed more than once, check to see if each listing is associated with the same sound house or studio.

- If more than one entry is listed with the same sound house or studio, call the entrant and notify him or her that only one entry is eligible.

- After the entrant has chosen the episode that he or she wishes to represent the sound house or studio in the competition, code the ineligibles as "I" and write "Multiple entries for same series—[name or entrant] opted for entry # [write in the entry number]." Then note your initials and the date.

- Refund entry fees for disqualified entry or entries. Enclose a refund request form so that the recipient will have written confirmation that the entry has been disqualified.

Once all the entries are in and the proofing has been done, it is time to prepare the ballots so Emmy voters can vote for the nominees. (Remember, this is a two-tier voting process. Voters first vote for nominees. Then the top five vote-getters go on a second ballot, and voters select a winner in each category.)

The ballots sent to the Emmy voters are an edited and reformatted version of the proofed and corrected entry information that is stored in the computer database.

If you have gone to all the trouble of entering the information off your entries into a database and proofing them meticulously, you should do as the Television Academy does and have the ballots printed directly from the information in the database. Under no circumstances should that information be transcribed. The same sorts of errors that have been purged during the proofing process inevitably will creep back into the data if it is transcribed.

Here is a sample page from the 1995 Emmy Awards Program Ballot. The Comedy Series entries that are listed were programmed by the computer to migrate from the database to this ballot page by two identifying marks:

- their category number, which designates them and only them as Comedy Series entries; and

- their eligibility code.

Only those entries coded as "R"—ready for the ballot—are allowed by the computer onto this ballot page. Those that were coded "I"—ineligible—are not allowed out of the database. It is very important that ineligible entries do not appear on the ballot, because the voters are limited to five votes per category. If an ineligible entry were listed, a vote cast for it would be a wasted vote.

Outstanding Comedy Series
Vote for no more than five programs in this category.

001	*All American Girl*
002	*Boy Meets World*
003	*Coach*
004	*Cybill*
005	*Dave's World*
006	*Double Rush*
007	*Dream On*
008	*Ellen*

[And so on, to the end of the category.]

Ballot Distribution and Return Audits

The distribution of ballots to a narrow-based electorate is comparable to stocking a corner grocery. The distribution of ballots to a broad-based electorate is comparable to stocking a supermarket.

For instance, the 275 to 300 art directors whose votes determine the Oscar art direction nominations are less than 5 percent of the approximately 7,000 AMPAS voters who determine the art direction winner—and each of those 7,000 voters obviously will need to receive a ballot.

Because broad-based ballots go to a relatively large

universe of voters, they typically are mailed. The voters then mark them and return them in some way that identifies them as legitimate.

To prove their legitimacy, ballots for magazine-sponsored awards usually must be an actual page torn from the magazine. Photocopies are not counted. (Clearly, people still could vote more than once by buying additional copies of the magazine, but that is something few publishers would discourage.)

In the case of the Emmys, each ballot is accompanied by a return envelope that is coded. The accountants who receive the ballot in that envelope will use the code for verification of legitimacy.

Problems can arise after the ballots have been distributed by mail to the voters. For example, if one member of the Academy calls and says he did not receive his ballot, the Academy will issue him a new ballot and a replacement return envelope with a new number. Then it will notify the accountants that the old number is invalid and the new number is legitimate.

This is to prevent the member from voting twice. But if, by some chance, that member later finds his first ballot, marks it and sends it to the accountants in its return envelope—instead of the second ballot—the accountants will not count it.

Naturally, you need to make such policies clear to voters, who might very innocently mail in the first ballot if they find it, then throw away the new one—and their vote.

A vital part of any awards procedure is determining how—or if—you will break ties. If you have de-

Dealing With Ties

cided that you will give out three awards if three candidates get the same number of votes, breaking a tie is a non-issue.

But if you will give only one award in each category, you'll need to be prepared for all kinds of eventualities.

You'll want to start determining the nominees or winners for a top vote-getter competition by stacking the voting results in descending order—from top vote-getter down to lowest vote-getter. For instance:

Entrant	Number of Votes
Bob	20
Linda	18
Sally	16
Tom	14
Roy	13

etc.

In the competition rules and procedures, you will need to note the ideal number of nominees. For example: "In each category of competition, there will ideally be three nominees." Therefore, the nominees in the above example are Bob, Linda and Sally.

If there is a tie vote in the stack that disallows the ideal number of nominees, competition rules must determine how the tie will be handled. For example, if Tom had received 16 votes, the rules would have to designate whether only Bob and Linda would be named as nominees—or whether Bob, Linda, Sally and Tom would all emerge as nominees. Or you may need a procedure for breaking the tie between Sally and Tom.

You could write a rule stating that "ties equidistant from the ideal number will always be settled by taking the higher number." Then there would be four nominees.

If the rule was that "ties equidistant from the ideal number will always be settled by taking the lower number," then there would be two nominees.

If the above ties were not equidistant from the ideal number—e.g., if Roy and Tom each had 16 votes, then the rule would have to provide for a choice of only a Bob-Linda field of nominees or a Bob-Linda-Sally-Tom-Roy field of nominees.

If the rule was that "ties not equidistant from the ideal number will always be settled by taking the number closest to the ideal number," then Bob and Linda would be the only nominees—i.e., in a choice of two or five nominees, two is closer to three and therefore is the number required by the rules.

Ties in a Rating System

Not all nominating systems are based on raw votes, of course. The National Information Infrastructure Awards have a ratings-score system.

There are three judging criteria under which judges rate the entries with point scores:

1) Capability (score entrant 1-10, 10 being best)

2) Results (score entrant 1-10, 10 being best)

3) Innovation (score entrant 1-10, 10 being best)

Total possible points: 30

If two entries receive the same number of total points, the tie is broken by choosing the entry with the higher score for Rating Criteria 1.

If the Rating Criteria 1 points are the same, the tie is broken by means of the highest score in Rating Criteria 2. If the points are the same in 2, the tie is broken by the high score in 3.

If the tie cannot be broken by the above means, the tied entries are submitted to the chairs of the ratings panel, which re-votes for 1. If the new votes do not break the tie, the process is repeated for Rating Criteria 2 and, if necessary, 3.

Ties in a Preferential Voting Format

Candidates are ranked by judges in a preferential voting format (such that the candidate most preferred by the voter gets a "1," the candidate liked second-best gets a "2," and so on until a preference number has been assigned to all candidates). As with a golf score, the lowest score wins.

Ties that occur in preferential voting systems can be broken via a statistical sampling. In order to break a tie, you would look for the entry that received the most "1" votes. If the tied entries had the same number of "1" votes, then you'd have to look for the entry with the most "2" votes, and so on, until the tie is broken. (The Emmy accountants consider a tie that is not broken after counting the "2" votes to be a statistical dead heat, and they leave the tie unbroken.)

In yet another variation on the above tie-breaking methods, the American Comedy Awards breaks ties by randomly factoring in scores that were submitted after the deadline for voting. "Dead" votes that otherwise would not be counted are added to the voting universe on a "blind draw" basis until the tie is broken.

Yet another approach is used by the American National Standards Institute. It allows the judges to create their choice of a third category of evaluation and use those additional ratings-score points to break the deadlocked scores from categories one and two.

In the Emmy Award proceedings, once the ballots are in, the ties have been broken and the top five vote-getters in each category have been determined, it's time for the final step in processing entries: preparing a press release to announce the nominees. (For more information on press releases, see Chapter 14, "How to Use Awards to Generate Publicity.")

On the timeline of an awards calendar, the announcement of the nominees comes at a predetermined date and time—after the entry period and before the announcement of the winners. It marks the second of three separations of the ordinary from the extraordinary in the awards process:

1) The first separation is the exclusion of would-be but ineligible entrants.

2) The second separation is the segregation of nominees from the rest of the entrants.

3) The third separation is the ascendancy of the winner(s) above the field of nominees.

The announcement of nominations should be in written form—normally a press release. They also may be announced "live." A sample of a Primetime Emmy

Awards press release cover sheet announcing the nominations appears in Appendix 4.

Notifying the Nominees

The notification of the nominees should be simultaneous with the announcement of the nominations. If there is a relatively small group of nominees, a phone call or telegram from the president of the organization is the preferable means of notification. If there are numerous nominees, they should be notified by mail.

However they are notified, nominees should receive written materials confirming their nomination, as well as details about the awards presentation. These include:

- a personalized letter of congratulations from the president of the organization;

- a personalized certificate of nomination;

- a request for additional information useful to the judges who will determine the winner(s);

- a printed invitation to the awards presentation;

- a complimentary R.S.V.P.—generally two free tickets for each nominee; and

- the name and phone number of a contact person at the organization who can answer any questions.

A particularly nice touch is enclosing a certificate of nomination suitable for framing. The certificate of nomination generally contains five standard elements:

- the name of the association sponsoring the awards;

- the name of the award;

- the name of the nominee;

- the date of the nomination; and

- the name and signature of the president of the association.

A request for additional material that will be used by the judges to determine the winner(s) should be sent in the same package as the nomination announcement. For example, here is a call for written scripts from the writer Emmy Award nominees:

Call for Nominated Emmy Awards Scripts

Scripts for the Outstanding Writing Categories

Nominated writing achievements in the comedy series and the miniseries/special categories will be screened at the Blue Ribbon Panels on August 12-13. In addition to viewing the telecast, the judges will be asked to read the writer's choice of his/her best script version of the telecast.

Please send a single copy of the script to the Academy by August 3. It will be duplicated, along with the other nominated scripts in the category, and sent to the panelists.

The Winners

For those of you whose awards programs are of the single-tier variety—where the candidate who gets the most votes wins—you would be more or less done at this point. You'd tally the votes, break any ties and have your winners. However, you still might want to build up some suspense before—and some interest in—your awards presentation by notifying the top five (or four or three) nominees, and keeping the winners secret until the presentation event. This also gives the nominees a chance to promote their nominations for the award, making it even more valuable to them and to you.

If you will be using a two-tier system, now is the time to separate the winners from the nominees by another round of voting or by jury.

For the final round of judging in the Emmys, the judging panels view the nominees' tapes, and the winners are determined.

The accountants then tabulate the votes and safeguard this information, so that the winners are not revealed until during the awards presentation ceremony. The accountants also prepare the final press release announcing the winners, which is distributed after the awards ceremony.

Post Mortem

After all is said and done, it usually is necessary to have a Post Mortem. This is a meeting (or a series of meetings) at which the principal administrators of the awards process review the hits, runs and errors of the competition and awards presentation.

The agenda should be subdivided into the key elements of the the awards process:

1) Rules and Procedures

2) Calendar (also, set the calendar for the next awards presentation)

3) Budget

4) Entries

5) Judging

6) Nominations

7) Awards Presentation

The Post Mortem should be a scheduled part of the process, just like the creation of ballots and the announcement of winners. We go into scheduling in more detail in the next chapter.

12

Time and Money

If you're running a business these days, you're probably running pretty lean. In the wake of downsizing and outsourcing, not many companies have a few spare people sitting around who have nothing better to do than devote all their time to putting together an awards program.

On the other hand, if you've read this far, you know the benefits from such programs can be invaluable. It should be well worth the effort and the expense to produce an awards program—even if that means squeezing the money for it out of your company's marketing or promotions budget. You may even be able to draft personnel from this department—or hire a consultant, if need be—to get the ball rolling. (Temps certainly would be able to input the entries into a database, and probably even take care of the proofing process.)

Obviously, figuring out how much an awards program is going to cost—or creating one to fit your budget—is a vital part of the planning process. So is setting up the awards calendar, which determines when the call for entries will be made, when the ballots will be mailed, when the awards presentation will take place and so on.

Let's start with the calendar, which should be the easier part of the process, then move on to the dollars and sense.

Using Rules and Procedures to Set the Awards Calendar

For some awards, timing is critical. For instance, if you are presenting a major industry award, you may want to schedule the presentation to occur during an industry trade show or convention. Similarly, the 1996 *Car Craft* All-Star Drag Racing Team awards were handed out the night before the 1997 NHRA drag racing season began, when the teams, sponsors and manufacturers had all converged on Pomona, California, anyway.

If you know the award's presentation date, you will need to set the awards calendar by calculating backward—so the awards process will be completed and the awards will be ready for presentation on schedule.

There are four parts to the procedure to set the awards calendar:

1) Identify the major steps in the awards process.

2) Calculate how much time it will take to complete each step.

3) Determine the total amount of time it takes to complete the process by adding up how much time it will take to complete each step.

4) Determine the date that the process is to begin by calculating backward from the date that the awards are to be presented.

As an example of how to identify the major steps in an awards process, let's again consider the Primetime Emmys. (Your process may have significantly fewer steps.)

Step 1: The Awards Committee reviews the prior year's rules. The Awards Committee is composed of two appointed representatives from each of the 24 branches of the Academy (writers, directors, performers, etc.). They review the problems that occurred during the prior year's Emmys and propose new rules or revise old ones in order to improve the competition.

Step 2: The Board of Governors ratifies the Awards Committee's proposals. The Board of Governors is composed of two elected representatives from each of the 24 branches of the Academy. They have final authority to approve new Emmy rules and changes.

Step 3: Distribution of entry forms. People who wish to compete fill out the forms and send them back to the Academy, where they are verified and placed on appropriate ballots (e.g., a ballot for the program entries, a ballot for the directors' entries, a ballot for the writers' entries, etc.).

Step 4: Nominating ballots are mailed to the members of the Academy. All members receive the Program Ballot (listing the entries for Comedy Series Programs, Drama Series Programs, etc.). Qualified members of different peer groups receive their peer group ballots—e.g., writers receive the Writing Ballot, directors the Directing Ballot, etc.

Step 5: Deadline for returning the voting cards to the accountants, who tabulate the votes. Generally, the top five vote-getters in each category of competition emerge as the nominees.

Step 6: Nominations are announced at a press conference at the Academy's Los Angeles headquarters. Immediately thereafter, nominees are asked to prepare tapes to be shown to the Emmy Judging Panels, where the winners will be determined.

Step 7: Emmy Judging Panels determine the winners.

Step 8: Announcement of the winners at the awards presentation on the Primetime telecast. In order to present Emmys to the winners on September 8, 1996, the nominees must be judged at the Emmy Judging Panels, and the accountants must have enough time to tabulate the votes and prepare for the announcement.

Calculating the Time Required for Each Step

In the case of the Emmys, the time estimates break down as follows:

Step 1: Total estimated time from the appointment of the Awards Committee to the completion of their rules review and its presentation to the Board of Governors: 12 weeks.

Step 2: Total estimated time from the Board of Governors ratification of the rules to the preparation and distribution of entry forms: 2 weeks.

Step 3: Total estimated time from the distribution of the entry forms to the preparation and mailing of the ballots: 16 weeks.

Step 4: Total estimated time from the distribution of the ballots to the return of the voting cards to the accountants: 3 weeks.

Step 5: Total estimated time from the return of the voting cards to the completion of the tabulations and the preparation of the nomination announcement: 4 weeks.

Step 6: Total estimated time from the announcement of nominations to the completion of preparations for the Emmy Judging Panels: 3 weeks.

Step 7: Total estimated time from the Emmy Judging Panels to the Primetime telecast: 4 weeks.

The grand total: 44 weeks. (If your total adds up to more than a year, you may need to simply your procedures, or consider making it a biennial award!)

Remember: An awards calendar must have "wiggle room"—i.e., extra time to accommodate the special circumstances that inevitably crop up in the course of a judging process.

An example of why wiggle room is so important occurred during a recent Los Angeles area Emmy Awards:

Per an agreement between the New York and Los Angeles chapters, they judged each others' entries for local news broadcasting. The deadline for the New York judging of the Los Angeles categories was set for April 18, the very date that the New York awards administrator had scheduled the final panel.

All was going well—the panel was in session, the tapes were rolling—when the broadcast news profes-

Wiggle Room

sionals from the New York stations who were doing the judging suddenly heard their beepers going off all over the room. A big fire had broken out somewhere on their collective beats and their assignment editors demanded that they get there with their camera crews—immediately! Within minutes, the panelists had dispersed and the April 18 deadline came and went without the judging being completed.

Panicked calls from the Los Angeles accountants streamed into the Los Angeles Emmy office late that afternoon. Where were the faxed ballots from the New York Panel that they needed in order to complete the tabulations and prepare the press release announcing the nominations?

Yes, they could rearrange their tabulation schedule and extend the deadline a day, but if the ballots were not in by noon at the latest on April 19, the categories being judged would not make the press release scheduled to go to the printer on April 24.

If they were not in the press release, they would not be published with the other nominations in the trade and Los Angeles papers, which would not only be a personal disappointment to the nominees, but—within the media community in the media center of the world—a professional slight.

Having the Emmys associated in any way with a professional slight is not what the Emmys are supposed to be about. Their value is a perceived, intangible capital that would certainly not be ruined by the diminished press release, but would be diminished in turn.

As things worked out, the New York panelists reconvened on the morning of the 19th and the ballots were duly faxed to the accountants that afternoon.

The tabulations were completed and the press release was published with a complete roster of nominations.

But, because contingencies for special circumstances that would precipitate delays that would threaten the successful completion of judging by the deadline were not built into the awards schedule, the culmination of the first stage of the judging process almost came to grief.

The amount of time, well-padded with wiggle room, necessary to complete each step of the judging of the Emmy Engineering Awards is as follows:

- The president has one month to seek and appoint the chair.

- The chair has one month to seek and appoint committee members.

- Three of four committee meetings are scheduled over the course of two months.

- Committee recommendations are sent to the Board of Governors two weeks prior to the meeting at which they will be ratified.

The total amount of time the process takes is four and a half months. Note that the time necessary for the solicitation of entries—two months—is not factored in, because it is running concurrently with the first two steps. By the time the committee has its first meeting, the entries are in.

Setting the Start Date

Once you've determined how long the process will take and added in some wiggle room, it's easy to calculate backward from the date the awards are to be presented and determine the date the process is to begin.

For the Emmys, this would happen as follows: September 8, 1996 (awards presentation) minus the 44 weeks it takes to complete the awards process places the beginning of the awards process in late October 1995.

Then you can plan the awards calendar accordingly:

Step 1) Awards Committee review of the prior year's rules: Late October 1995

Step 2) Board of Governors ratification of the Awards Committee's proposals: Mid-January 1996

Step 3) Distribution of entry forms: Beginning of February

Step 4) Nominating ballots mailed: Beginning of June

Step 5) Deadline for returning voting cards to the accountants: Third week in June

Step 6) Nominations announced: Mid-July

Step 7) The Emmy Judging Panels: Second Week in August

Step 8) Primetime telecast: September 8, 1996

The Baldrige Awards calendar is set up in much the same way. It has seven steps, culminating in the announcement and presentation of the awards in late October of each year.

The Baldrige rules require that the following procedures be fulfilled within the course of the awards process:

• Applicants file an eligibility determination

form to establish their placement in one of three award categories.

- Applicants apply for an award in their appropriate category.

- The application is initially considered by members of the Board of Examiners, who recommend the best candidates to a consensus review. The best of those candidates move on to a site visit review, with the best of those candidates proffered to a final judges' review. The Secretary of Commerce makes the last review and determines the awards recipients.

Like the Emmys, the Baldrige cycle takes about 10 months to complete (January to October). If you were setting up the calendar for this awards cycle, you would work backward from the awards presentation and create a calendar as follows:

Step 7: Announcement/Presentation. The end date for the awards cycle is late October, when the awards are announced and presented by the president of the United States at a ceremony in Washington, D.C.

Step 6: Final Judging. From the date of the awards presentation, back up approximately one month to early October and block about 3 weeks for the judges' final review of candidates (approximately October 1-21).

Step 5: Site Visit Review. From the date on which the final judging begins, back up approximately one month to early September, and block about three weeks for the site visit review. In 1996, the small business review was September 2-7; the manufacturing review, September 8-14; the service sector review, September 15-21.

Step 4: Consensus Review. Back up to early June and block June, July and August for this review.

Step 3: Independent Review. Back up to early April and block April and May for this review.

Step 2: Award Application. Back up to early March and block the month of March to complete and submit award applications.

Step 1: Eligibility Determination. Back up to the first of the year, and prepare the Eligibility Determination Package no later than March 1.

The National Association of Broadcasters generally holds its first committee meeting in early May—after the rollout of the latest technical products at the National Association of Broadcasters convention.

In order to have the chair and committee in place by early May, the awards administrator must notify the president that he or she needs to appoint a committee chair by early March.

If the committee takes two months to complete its deliberations, it will finish in early July.

Its recommendations are sent to the board, which meets two weeks later for ratification. The awards are announced the day after the board meeting—approximately July 15.

In summary, the four-and-a-half-month process is calendared as follows:

- The president has one month to seek and appoint the chair: During March

- The chair has one month to seek and appoint committee members: During April

- Three of four committee meetings are scheduled over the course of two months: During May and June

- Committee recommendations are sent to the Board of Governors two weeks prior to the meeting at which they will be ratified: During the first week in July

- The winners are announced the day after the board's monthly meeting: In Mid-July

Using Rules and Procedures to Set the Awards Budget

While timing is critical in an awards process, all the time in the world won't make up for an inadequate budget. Here's how to figure out what you'll need, financially speaking, for your awards program.

First, remember that there are three categories of income and expenditures that make up an awards budget:

- pre-awards;

- awards; and

- post-awards.

Income

While recognition awards typically do not garner income, all of the other forms of awards we discussed in this book do bring in some money before, during and often after the awards presentation event.

Charity awards are fundraisers and are planned to produce—ideally in the short run, and definitely in the long term—a surplus of income over expenditures.

An example of *pre-awards income* in a charity award would be an amount pledged for sponsorship of the money-generating event (e.g., the Widget Co. pledges $10,000 for overall, unencumbered sponsorship of the Angel Awards).

Awards income for a charity award typically would be money raised in ticket sales, program-book ad sales and receipts from a silent auction held on the night of the awards gala.

Post-awards income for charities is typically in the form of contributions made after the awards gala by people who attended and were impressed enough by the charity and the proceedings to send in their checks when contacted in a follow-up solicitation.

Associations may realize a cash surplus on their awards, but because they generally are nonprofit, they look at a break-even rather than a profitable bottom line. At any rate, the money is secondary to the two reasons associations have awards:

1) to represent the professional purpose of their parent association;

2) to further the goals of the association and reflect its values.

An example of pre-awards income in the Primetime Emmys is the annual licensing fee that the Academy receives from the network that will be broadcasting the show. It is a pre-negotiated amount that stands apart from income generated from fees and other monies paid by the participants during the competition itself (awards income) and by the nominees and winners for certificates and commemorative statues after the competition is completed (post-awards income).

Baldrige pre-award funding comes from:

- the Foundation for the Malcolm Baldrige Awards, which contributes more than $600,000 annually for the administration of the awards. The foundation's contribution is capitalized through donations made by about 150 companies to an endowment that amounts to more than $10 million.

- the federal government, which antes up approximately $5 million per annum to cover administrative costs.

Awards income for association awards comes mainly from entry fees. For instance, to enter the Baldrige Awards, large businesses pay $4,500 and small businesses give $1,500. The entry fees for the competitive categories of the Primetime Emmys generally are scheduled according to the number of entrants. For instance, a single entrant (such as a performer) pays $100 per entry, whereas a team of four sound mixers pays $200 per entry, and a team of 12 sound editors pays $400 per entry. As with most association entry fees, all or part of the fee is waived for members.

Associations also may ask businesses to sponsor the awards program—or the awards presentation event. (Sponsorships usually include a certain number of seats or tables at the awards presentation event.) For instance, a record 31 companies sponsored the 1996 awards event for the Society of Plastics Engineers (SPE) Automotive Division. The sponsorship money is used to fund SPE scholarships and technical seminars. The group also charged $65 for tickets to the awards banquet.

Associations may generate post-awards income by selling commemorative certificates to the award winners, who distribute them to people or companies who materially contributed to the award-winning achievement. However, these usually are provided at the association's cost and are not considered a profit center.

Entry Fees

Entry fees for competitive awards have two purposes:

- to generate income to offset expenditures; and

- to discourage an excessive number of entries.

Up to 1988, the Primetime Emmy Awards did not charge entry fees for performers' entries. But the increase in original programming brought about by the ever-expanding cable television networks, the new Fox Network and the burgeoning first-run syndication business led to a proportionate increase in the number of performer entries. By 1987, there were 1,550 entries on the Performer Ballot. (These included all entries for lead and supporting male and female actors in comedy, drama, variety-music, miniseries and TV movies.)

Further pushing up the number of entries was the incorrect but widely held opinion in the television industry that having one's name listed on a ballot was tantamount to being nominated. People who called the Academy for information would typically ask, "How can I nominate myself for an Emmy?" when they really meant to ask, "How can I enter the competition?" What they were told was that any eligible individual could make an entry and be placed on the appropriate ballot, which was nothing more than a roster of like-minded individuals vying for votes.

Only after the ballots were sent to the Academy membership—the voters—and the accountants had tallied the resulting votes, would the top five vote-getters in each category be separated out from the entrants and named as nominees.

The process was not too complicated and, deep down, people understood that being on the ballot did not imply Academy recognition. But, in their hearts, they sensed that if television was a business culture where publicity and "being seen" were thought to be fundamental to survival (if not success), then they ought to have their names or program titles listed on the Emmy ballot.

Besides, if they had not fully understood the distinction between an entry and a nomination, others might make the same error!

And even if they didn't, the entry was free, so nothing was lost, right?

Wrong. What was being lost was the average Emmy voter, who did not have the time or patience to "read the 'phonebook,'" as the Performer Ballot came to be known. Complaints reached the Board of Governors, and they decided to impose an entry fee in order to make those who would use the ballots as an advertisement for themselves think twice before they placed their next ad. The board imposed an entry fee of $75.

It worked. Entries on the Performer Ballot dropped 50 percent, from 1,550 to 780.

A valid concern with regard to entry fees: Does the quality of the competition diminish along with the quantity of entries?

The Academy tested that question by comparing the no-fee nominations with those nominated during the first year of the fee. Here are comparisons of the Lead Actress in a Comedy Series and Supporting Actor in a Comedy Series categories:

Lead Actress in a Comedy Series— 1987 Nominations (no fee)

- Bea Arthur (*The Golden Girls*)
- Blair Brown (*The Days and Nights of Molly Dodd*)
- Jane Curtin (*Kate & Allie*)
- Rue McClanahan (*The Golden Girls*)
- Betty White (*The Golden Girls*)

Lead Actress in a Comedy Series— 1988 Nominations (fee)

- Kirstie Alley (*Cheers*)
- Bea Arthur (*The Golden Girls*)
- Blair Brown (*The Days and Nights of Molly Dodd*)
- Rue McClanahan (*The Golden Girls*)
- Betty White (*The Golden Girls*)

Four of the five pre-entry fee nominees returned in the first year that the entry fee was imposed. The fifth nominee, Jane Curtin, could not have been nominated, because *Kate & Allie* was off the air.

As for the supporting men:

Supporting Actor in a Comedy Series— 1987 Nominations (no fee)

- Woody Harrelson (*Cheers*)
- John Larroquette (*Night Court*)
- Tom Poston (*Newhart*)
- Peter Scolari (*Newhart*)
- George Wendt (*Cheers*)

Supporting Actor in a Comedy Series— 1988 Nominations (fee)

- Kelsey Grammer (*Cheers*)
- Woody Harrelson (*Cheers*)
- John Larroquette (*Night Court*)
- Peter Scolari (*Newhart*)
- George Wendt (*Cheers*)

Once again, four of the five pre-entry fee nominees returned in the first year that the entry fee was imposed. (The fifth nominee for the "fee year" was Kelsey Grammer, who debuted on *Cheers* in 1988 with such a splash that he edged out Tom Poston, who had been nominated for *Newhart* the prior two years in a row.)

The review showed that even though the ranks of the entrants had been thinned out by nearly 50 percent, the ranks of the nominees remained relatively unchanged. The voters continued to nominate laudable, competitive entrants, almost as if nothing had changed but the thickness of "the phone book."

Clearly, there's merit in charging entry fees—as long as the fee will not impose an unbearable burden on entrants. You may want to consider charging a fee for your awards program, particularly if you have a large pool of possible entrants. Your judges will thank you for it.

Expenditures

While you may not have associated the awards process with income, surely you expected some expenditures to be involved, even for something as simple as a Good Egg Award.

Specific types of expenditures are connected with each phase of the awards process. The following checklist covers a wide range of possibilities that may or may not be applicable to every awards program.

Pre-Awards Expenditures
Awards Committee Meetings

- hotel
- meals
- transportation reimbursements
- phone cost of conference calls

Printing

- publicity/informational press releases
- entry forms
- rules and procedures brochures or booklets

Postage and Delivery

- awards committee communications
- distribution of publicity materials
- distribution of competition materials

Awards Expenditures

Judging

- hotel
- meals
- transportation reimbursements
- phone cost of conference calls

Printing

- ballots and other judging materials
- publicity/informational press releases
- communications with entrants
- awards presentation invitations
- awards presentation tickets
- awards presentation program book
- awards presentation auction materials
- nomination/winner certificates (along with folders for their presentation)

Postage and Delivery

- awards committee communications
- distribution of ballots and other judging materials

- distribution of publicity/informational materials

- distribution of communications with competition participants

- delivery of auction materials to and from awards presentation

Awards Presentation Production

- preparation of audio-visual materials (taping, editing, film transfers, etc.)

Awards Presentation

- awards (trophy, loving cup, etc.)

- venue (hotel/hall, gratuities, parking)

- food and beverages

- staff (wages, clothing and transportation reimbursements)

- room prep (stage, backstage, special accommodations)

- audio-visual (spotlights, projectors, tape players, tape recorders, cameras, screens)

- decorations (table and stage)

- auction (display cases/tables)

Post-Awards Expenditures

Printing

- publicity/informational press releases

- additional certificates

Postage and Delivery

- distribution of publicity materials
- distribution of awards not picked up at the awards presentation

Miscellaneous

- trophy engraving

Should You Pay the Judges?

Although accountants do not formally recognize the adage, "A penny saved is a penny earned," volunteer contributions to an awards process defer significant expenditures.

For example, if the Television Academy were to pay the hourly rate for the judges who give freely of their time and expertise to determine both the Emmy nominees and the winners, the costs would be in the tens of millions of dollars. The administrator of the Baldrige Awards estimates that the value of the services of the executives who evaluate the candidates exceeds $6 million per year.

Judges' expenses should be paid, but judges should not. This is analogous to the situation of criminal and civil jurors at the local courthouse, who are not so much "paid" as reimbursed for their mileage and incidental expenses.

Admittedly, courthouse jurors are compelled to serve. But by donating their time and their honest evaluation of case evidence, they also show at least tacit support for the system of justice that calls them to service and the larger society that sanctions it.

Similarly, awards juries are "called"—as the rules

of the competition identify them as competent to evaluate the candidates against the criteria. They agree to serve because they support the awards program (a.k.a. the "system of justice") and the mission (a.k.a. "the larger society") that it fulfills. As with courthouse jurors, their payment is an inherent intangible that comes with their participation.

Getting to the Bottom Line

Recognition awards are meant to be a formal recognition of both the subjective and objective achievements of company employees. Designed to generate morale and good will within the company, they are planned as debit items.

On the other hand, company awards, such as the Baldrige Award, may or may not create a surplus of income over expenditures, depending on one's point of view. From a strict financial accounting viewpoint, the Baldrige Awards' expenditures are significantly greater than their actual cash income. But, according to a report presented to the U.S. Senate, every dollar spent on the administration of the award returns $97 to the awards process in "support from industry."

This surplus, in turn, establishes an endowment of total quality management from which the Baldrige Awards participants generate the added value of learning and sharing best business practices among themselves. In its summary statement for 1995, the Baldrige criteria booklet stated that the learning/sharing component of the awards:

> far exceeds expectations and program requirements. Award winners' efforts have encouraged many other organizations in all sectors of the U.S.

economy to undertake their own performance improvement efforts.

Notes Pat Mene, TQM head at the Ritz Carlton hotel headquarters in Atlanta, "The awarding of the Baldrige Award to one company is just the beginning of the process that makes the award so valuable to many companies."

Or as the report to the U.S. House of Representatives said:

> The life blood of the award is the energy it has unleashed in thousands of volunteers, in the award-winning companies and others. Their efforts over the years translate into many hundreds of millions of dollars of benefits to the U.S. ... The Baldrige Award is about understanding and facilitating the sharing of the practices that enable the major gains the award winners have demonstrated.

The bottom line effects of this concerted boost in business productivity are demonstrated through a hypothetical investment experiment. According to an NIST report in May 1996:

> An investment in each of the publicly traded Baldrige winners from the first business day in April in the year the company won the award until August 1995 yielded a 248.7 percent return on investment, compared with a 58 percent return for the Standard & Poor's 500 index, thus outperforming the S&P 500 by more than 4 to 1.

13

The Awards Presentation

When McCaw Cellular Communications was just starting out, the company couldn't afford to pay its employees much. But founder Craig McCaw looked for other ways to motivate them—and build loyalty. He decided to launch an awards program, which he called the Circle of Excellence.

To increase the value of the award, employees had to be nominated by their peers for doing outstanding work. Winners received a trip to Hawaii or the Bahamas.

But they weren't just handed a ticket and given a pat on the back. To emphasize the importance of the award—and the behavior it encouraged—McCaw held a fancy banquet at which the winners were recognized and the awards were presented. Craig McCaw and all of the top managers attended. Their presence added an element of respect that should always be the purpose and hallmark of an awards presentation. While the vacations and the fine dining were important tangible rewards, the celebration of excellence at which they were delivered added inestimable value.

The planning for every awards presentation, be it part of a convention luncheon or an Emmy Awards telecast, should begin with the question:

Planning the
Awards
Presentation

"How many people will attend?"

The answer to that question begs the next: "What facility will accommodate the number of people who will attend?"

Which leads to the third question: "Is it in the budget?"

The fourth question is whether the preferred facility that will accommodate the attendees is available at the preferred date and time of the event.

And the fifth question that should be asked is whether the awards presentation will occur on the coattails of another event or be a free-standing presentation.

If the awards presentation is part of the program of a convention-ending luncheon that will be held in the convention hotel, and the luncheon is for 600 people, and the only room in the hotel that will seat 600 is the main ballroom, then the "how many, where, how much, when and what" questions have been easily answered.

However, if you are not tied to a convention facility, the choices can be almost overwhelming. Should you have the presentation at your company's headquarters? a hotel? a restaurant? Do you want to make a statement with your choice of location?

Is there a site that will make people want to attend your awards presentation—above and beyond their interest in finding out who won the awards? The staff at Petersen Publishing Co. was able to find such a site for the 1996 *Car Craft* All-Star Drag Racing Awards— and it was located right down the street from the magazines' offices. The place: the Petersen Automotive Museum (named after the founder of the publishing company, who donated the money to purchase the facility and renovate it). The museum is filled with significant race cars, street cars and other interesting exhibits that made the awards presentation even more of an event for the numerous drag racing teams, sponsors and manufacturers who had come to L.A. from other parts of the country.

By the same token, a group giving out environmentally oriented awards might want to do so at a site that overlooks the ocean or a lake or river.

Choosing the right awards presentation site can even add to the perceived value of the awards themselves. Conversely, giving them out at a site that is too small or doesn't have sufficient seating—or that doesn't have an adequate sound system—actually can devalue the awards being presented.

There are three elements common to most awards presentations:

- People getting awards;
- People giving awards; and
- The awards themselves.

There are another two elements that can be added as variations on—or embellishments to—the above:

- audio-visual presentation; and
- talent/entertainment.

Elements of the Awards Presentation

While we normally think of big awards presentations as something reserved for charities trying to raise money—and entertainment industry functions, à la the

Business Awards Presentations

Emmys and the Oscars—businesses don't have to have boring awards presentations. Even a presentation that is part of a larger event (such as a convention-ending luncheon) or a presentation that occurs during normal business hours can still include some of the embellishments for awards presentations.

For instance, consider the hypothetical Good Egg Award. President Widget could simply invite Betty from accounts payable up to a board meeting in the conference room, where she is handed the award, stammers her thanks and leaves. Or the Widget Co. could make it a larger, more memorable and more enjoyable event.

Let's assume that the Widget Co. has decided to stage a nice presentation for Betty. Here's how the pre-production process would go.

Awards Presentation Pre-Production

The first step toward putting on an awards presentation is making the pre-production checklist. It is a guide to the awards presentation based on:

- the "how many, where, how much, when and what" questions;

- plus the three basic awards presentation elements (people getting awards, people giving awards and the awards themselves);

- and the two additional elements (audio-visual presentation and talent/entertainment).

For the Good Egg Award, the checklist would be:

Award Title
The Good Egg Award

How Many in Attendance
20 Widget Co. board members
3 staff reps
Betty from accounts receivable (recipient)
Betty's supervisor
Betty's supervisor's supervisor
Bob from support services (a-v technician)
Total: 26

Where
The Widget Co. board room

How Much
Cost of Good Egg trophy with engraving: $55
(pre-budgeted through the Widget Co.'s General
& Administrative Slush Fund)

When
June 21, 1996
6 p.m. reception
6:30 p.m. dinner
7:30 p.m. award presentation
Board meeting to follow

What
Business-based subjective recognition award

People Getting Award
Betty from accounts receivable

People Giving Award
The Good Egg Award is given by the board of
directors.

And the Winner Is ...   257

Mr. Widget is the presenter.

The Award Itself
A golden egg mounted atop a granite block with "To Betty, A Good Egg" engraved on it

Audio-Visual
Videotape: A VHS tape running approximately 3 minutes from the president of the Angel Awards, thanking the Widget Co. for donating its Christmas Party Fund money to Charity X for research leading to the cure of Disease Y. Special thanks to Betty and Mr. Widget and the board of directors.

Equipment: VHS playback deck and 19-inch monitor (located in boardroom a-v cabinet)

Technician: Bob from support services

Talent/Entertainment
The Widget Co. Glee Club singing *The Wind Beneath My Wings* (a cappella)

Presentation Mode
Following dinner, the board chair will:

- Welcome Betty

- Welcome Betty's supervisor

- Welcome Betty's supervisor's supervisor

- Describe the award and the awards process

- Introduce Mr. Widget

- Mr. Widget congratulates Betty, then introduces the Angel Award tape

- Roll tape

- Mr. Widget introduces the glee club

- The Widget Co. Glee Club enters the board
  room and sings *The Wind Beneath My Wings*
  to Betty

- Betty accepts the award

- Betty, supervisors, Bob and glee club exit so
  board can begin meeting

Respect is the key intangible in a successful awards presentation. And the "small details" of its organization make that respect manifest.

The Terryberry Co.'s guidelines for an in-house awards presentation illustrate the concept:

- Make sure you have the right awards for each
  of the recipients, and that all details of the
  award are correct.

- Arrange the awards in the order they are to
  be presented—and, if they are in boxes, label
  them.

- Have an assistant who can hand the award
  to the presenter. If there are many awards to
  be presented, it may be more efficient to have
  assistants deliver the awards to winners who
  remain where they are seated or standing.
  Highlight these winners with a spotlight or,
  if budget permits, capture the recipient on
  camera and project the image onto a large
  screen in the front of the room.

And the Winner Is ...

- If winners are to come forward to receive their award, make sure to arrange seating to facilitate easy access to the staging area.

- Put the recipients at ease by making them feel appreciated and honored as individuals. Personal anecdotes and stories about the recipients and their co-workers will help everyone relax. Stories about the award recipient and other employees in the department are appropriate, along with the relationship of that department to the entire organization and its accomplishments.

Terryberry also offers some valuable advice regarding hosts, speakers and topics:

- Service awards may be introduced by the CEO or a master of ceremonies, who speaks about the importance of long-term employees and employer stability.

- The person who presents the award is often the recipient's immediate supervisor or manager. It is important that the presenter be someone who knows the recipient well enough to be fully comfortable explaining the recipient's achievements.

- Sales awards should focus on the sales team, as well as the individual winners.

- An executive can introduce the awards with comments about the team's hard work, challenges that have been met, customers and competition. Individual awards then highlight the contributions of the winners and their personal achievements.

A "special event" awards presentation typically incorporates most of the additional elements of awards presentations noted above. However, it is different from a "business-based" awards presentation because of two factors:

- rather than being contained within a larger event, it is the principal event;

- it occurs outside normal business hours and the context of ordinary business activities.

An example of a special event awards presentation is the Angel Awards:

- Every year, Charity X stages the Angel Awards to honor an individual or company that has made significant contributions toward the fight to end Disease Y.

- This year, the Widget Co., whose employees opted to donate to Charity X the money set aside for their annual Christmas party, is chosen for the award.

- The awards are scheduled for the ballroom of a nice hotel. Tickets are sold for an evening of dinner, dancing, a silent auction, an appearance by a celebrity or two, and the principal event: the presentation of the award to the nice folks at the Widget Co.

The Primetime Emmy Awards and the Oscars are examples of very elaborate special event awards, but they differ only in degree and not in kind from the Angel Awards.

A sensitive issue in all awards presentations is the length of the acceptance speech. The recipient certainly should have the opportunity to express his or her feelings and give credit where it is due, but the stress, confusion and overwhelming emotions of the moment often reduce the winner to stammering incoherence or bovine silence. Indicative of that temporary insanity on-stage, the winner's recollection of the speech generally is vague or nil, only that, "He felt he was in the grip of some vertigo, hearing himself talking without consciously willing any words," as Kingsley Amis wrote in *Lucky Jim*.

To improve the awards ceremony—and to help everyone involved appear in their best light—awards nominees and recipients should be notified well in advance of the awards presentation that:

- they will have a certain amount of time (20 to 30 seconds is the time given to Emmy nominees) to give their speech;

- if there is a group of nominees or winners, a single spokesperson should be selected to speak on behalf of the group;

- they should have something in writing—either notes or a final draft—to assure that the speech will be complete and correct.

On the occasion of the 50th anniversary of the Television Academy, a film reel was put together featuring "Great Emmy Moments." Included was the shortest and yet the most complete acceptance speech on record:

Actress Lee Grant approached the podium, took her Emmy from the presenter and turned to the audience. When the enthusiastic applause finally died down, she said, "The feeling is mutual," and exited.

The basic tool of the awards production is the script. Although they may differ in format, all scripts embody the transformation of disparate ingredients (the pre-production checklist/guide) into a finished product (the awards presentation "show").

To give you an idea of how you might want to structure your script, we'll take a look at the script for the Sports Legends Awards. It begins with a title page that gives an at-a-glance review of the entire special event. Commentary and tips for putting together your awards presentation production appear in boldface italics.

The name of the awards
The Fifth Annual Sports Legends Awards

The date of the event
Thursday, April 11, 1996

The venue and rooms being used
Beverly Hills Hotel
Reception, dinner and awards presentation in the Crystal Ballroom
VIP reception in the Sunset Room
Interviews in the Rodeo Room

Awards
Presentation
Production

A short rundown of the awards presentation
Show Sequence
[Bob Miller Intro]
1. Amy Alcott
2. Ron Cey
3. Butch Goring
4. Pat McCormick
5. Kurt Rambis
6. Bill Shoemaker
7. [Don Newcombe & Rogie Vachon—plaque to Bob Miller, goodnight]

And the schedule for taping pre-show interviews:
VIP Room Interview Schedule:
5:30 p.m.   Amy Alcott
5:40 p.m.   Ron Cey
6:00 p.m.   Butch Goring
6:10 p.m.   Pat McCormick
6:20 p.m.   Kurt Rambis
6:30 p.m.   Bill Shoemaker

The script preface begins with a review of the positions that the show personnel must be in during the course of the awards presentation. Just as in a cooking recipe, the ingredients not only are listed, but they also are added to the mix in a specific sequence. The script must give specific information about who should be where at what time.

Script Preface
8 p.m.—Pre-Show Stage Left:
Julie Shore [Stage Manager]
Bob Miller

During Show—Stage Left:
Julie Shore [Stage Manager]
Bob Miller
Don Newcombe and Rogie Vachon (cue is Bill
Shoemaker Award)

At this special event, dinner is preceded by a re-
ception and silent auction outside the dining room.
Because there is an announcement being made by the
voice-over (V.O.) announcer for the show, this pre-
show part of the evening needs to be scripted.

At 6:40 p.m.,
- Open the doors to the dining room.

- Raise and lower the lights in the foyer.

- Announce that dinner will be served in just
  a few minutes.

- Request that people take their seats.

- Repeat as necessary.

Dinner served from 7 to approximately 8 p.m.

At 7:40,
V.O. announces that the silent auction will be concluded in 10 minutes.

Here is where the show script begins. The busi-
ness with the lights and the music goes on just long
enough to get the audience's attention.

Show Script

At 8 p.m.:

- Dim the house lights to show level.

- Rake the room with the follow spot.

- Bring up the show-opening music.

- And Bob Miller intro.

This awards presentation involves extensive audio-visual "feeds" to a large screen in the center of the room. In effect, the show is "live TV," except for the fact that it is not being transmitted anyplace other than the projection screen.

The video feeds are either pre-produced tape or the images from the live cameras in the room.

There are two cameras. Camera One is tripod-mounted on a riser in the back of the room and always aimed at the single podium on stage. Depending on what is going on, it will either be in a tight focus on the person at the podium or a wide shot of the entire stage. Camera Two is hand-held by an operator in the pit in front of the stage. It either feeds the podium action from a low angle, or it reverses for a shot of the audience or for a floor shot of people coming out of the house to the podium.

The technical director for the show sits at a video switcher in a control booth that is set off by pipe and drape in a corner of the room. He has a monitor for Camera One, another one for Camera Two and a third for the pre-produced video "roll-ins." He has yet another monitor that shows the "line feed"—i.e., what is projected to the stage screen. Through the course of the show, he feeds to the line Camera One, Camera Two or the roll-ins.

The first image on the screen is a video "roll in" of a tape of the Sports Legends Award—a silver loving cup mounted on a walnut base—revolving on a turntable. This tape was shot earlier in the day by one of the cameramen. In order to make the trophy look its best, he fitted his camera with a star filter lens that gave the light reflecting off the trophy a diamond-like sparkle. He got the turntable from a kitchen supply store—nothing more than a wind-up microwave turntable purchased for less than $20. He shot about 10 minutes of the spinning trophy, which he estimated would be more than sufficient for its repeated roll-ins. He labeled this **Tape #1—Spinning Trophy.**

Announcer (V.O.): "Good evening, ladies and gentlemen, and welcome to ..."
[Roll *Tape #1—Spinning Trophy.*]
"... the Fifth Annual Sports Legends Awards.
"Here is tonight's host, the television voice of the Los Angeles Kings, Bob Miller."

[Follow spot picks up Bob entering from stage left wings. He goes to the podium.]
[Cut opening music. Cut screen projection from spinning award to podium-cam shot of Bob.]

Bob: "Welcome to this evening of great sports legends.

"We have a very distinguished audience tonight! In case you didn't have a chance to meet and greet as much as you wanted to before dinner, here is a video vignette that surveys at least the less camera-shy of tonight's guests."

A standard part of the beginning portion of awards shows is the introduction of association officials, honored guests and other VIPs. Because this is awkward and technically difficult in a dimly lit venue, such as a hotel ballroom, the Camera Two operator went to the pre-dinner reception and asked the VIPs to look into the lens, smile and wave a greeting. No sound was recorded. The tape was "edited in the camera"— i.e., because he was just gathering a sequence of greetings, one after another, the tape could be shown just as it was shot.

Along with Camera Two was an association official who guided the operator to the VIPs and wrote down their names in the sequence they were taped. When the tape was shown, the voice-over announcer recited the names that went with the faces on the screen. Background music gave the sequence a produced feel.

Live V.O. announcer in synch with the sequence of attendees on the tape roll, with musical overlay. At end, project Bob back on screen and cut music.

Bob: "And now, ladies and gentlemen, I have the honor to present our first sports legend."

Dim room to projection level and kill podium spot. Roll spinning trophy tape for 5 to 7 seconds to focus the attention of the audience on the screen and provide a transition to the legend tape. Then roll tape on Amy Alcott. At the end of the tape, freeze-frame shot of Amy that appears at the end of the tape. Spotlight back on podium.

Bob asks the audience to welcome Amy.

Play vamp-to-stage music.

The follow spot picks up Amy, who comes to the stage from the house. Cut music. Bob gives her the trophy, steps back and waits for Amy to give her speech. When finished, she then exits back to the house.

In the above sequence of events, the line feed goes like this:

1. *Camera One (tight shot on Bob as he introduces Alcott clip)*

2. *Roll-in #1 (spinning trophy)*

3. *Roll-in #2 (Alcott tape)*

4. *Camera Two (on Amy as she comes out of the audience toward the podium)*

5. *Camera One (wide shot on Bob presenting Amy with the trophy)*

6. *Camera Two (low-angle tight shot on Amy giving speech interspersed with Camera One shots, both tight and medium)*

Without any introduction of the next legend, repeat above pattern for:

- Ron Cey
- Butch Goring
- Pat McCormick
- Kurt Rambis
- Bill Shoemaker

After Bill leaves the stage, cut to spinning trophy.

V.O. announcer intros Don Newcombe and Rogie Vachon.

V.O. announcer: "Please welcome the chair and vice chair of the Sports Legends Council, Dodger great Don Newcombe and [Bob's words] Rogie Vachon.

Don and Rogie enter from stage left.

Don and Rogie:
[They thank the audience for its support of the Paralysis Project. They thank Bob for doing a great job and call him on stage. They present him with a plaque.]

Bob, Don and Rogie:
[All three say goodnight.]

Roll:
Show credits
Spinning trophy

Play post-show music.

When credits end, bring lights up to pre-set level. Project spinning trophy and play music for about 15 minutes as the room clears, then cut both.

THE END

As you customize your awards presentation to celebrate excellence within your company or industry, you can add, subtract, multiply or divide the above example as you see fit. Just remember that the following elements are basic to your agenda:

- Welcome by the master of ceremonies (M.C.).

- Introductions by the M.C.

- Background on the organization and the purpose of its awards program.

- Description of awards and the criteria for selection.

- Introduction of nominees or recipients.

- Presentation of awards.

- Acceptances.

- Concluding remarks by the M.C.

Get It on Tape

The awards presentations should be recorded by means of audio tape, videotape, still photos or a combination of the three. The record is useful for archival purposes, but it also can be reconstituted as:

- a feature piece in the company or association newsletter or annual report;

- a nostalgic highlight reel for use in the next presentation of the awards;

- for a charity, a promotional piece designed to laud the work of the charity and help sell tables to the next awards presentation;

- for an association or a charity, a record of the evening that can be made available to the honored guests, nominees and winners as a free memento or for their purchase.

Post-Ceremony Personalization of the Awards

The distribution of the awards themselves occurs during the awards presentation, but there could be some post-production personalizing of the awards. For instance, you may want to engrave the names of the winners on the awards—something you couldn't do beforehand if you were going to have the awards on display before they were presented (unless there is no suspense involved, as in the Good Egg Award).

Because the Academy's accountants have sole knowledge of the identities of the winners before they are announced, the Emmys handed out at the awards are not personally engraved with the names and achievements of the recipients. For the first 33 years of the Emmys, the statuette was handed out on stage, and then immediately retrieved in the wings by the chair of the Awards Committee. The scripted remark to the winner was:

This is just a stage prop. Your Emmy will be personally engraved and sent to you in six to eight weeks. Congratulations!

The winner was usually so dazed that the statuette was surrendered without an argument.

But, occasionally, the disappointment of parting with the newly won treasure prompted fierce objections or sad stories. One winner said he had promised his sick mother that if he won, he would drive right over to her bedside to show her the prize. He had even cleared things with the hospital to get in after visiting hours. (Allowed to take the Emmy, he was seen shortly thereafter on the dance floor—award in hand—at the post-awards Governors Ball.)

In 1984, the Academy changed its policy and let every winner keep his or her Emmy. After the awards presentation, the trophy manufacturer (R.S. Owens in Chicago) would make up new bands and engrave them. Each winner then was sent his or her personalized band in six to eight weeks with instructions on how to install it—a process not unlike changing a light bulb. (The Academy staff is always available to change a band if the winner wishes.)

This is possible because the Emmy statuette is made up of four parts: the sculpture of the muse holding the atom; which is mounted atop a slightly convex plate that is etched with a grid that represents latitude and longitude, symbolizing the world; which is mounted atop a black-enameled brass engraving band; which is mounted atop a felt-bottomed plate that serves as the base. The four parts are joined by a bolt that extends from the bottom of the muse's feet, through a hole in the center of the grid, the open space of the band and a hole in the center of the base, where a nut joins it and, when tightened, secures the four parts.

Awards Presentation Do's and Don'ts

From inception to wrap-up, awards presentations have a multitude of variables that you must identify, prioritize and customize to your own ends.

Small, intimate awards presentations are less complicated to prepare and less costly to administer, but if they feel cramped and cheap, they will only diminish the importance of the awards.

Special event presentations are an opportunity to engage a large audience with the dramatic sizzle of showmanship, but they can become overblown and obnoxious to audience and recipients alike.

What to do?

Sociologist Abraham Maslow's observations on the hierarchy of human needs are useful here as both a practical and theoretical guideline for do's and don'ts at your awards presentation:

1) Food, shelter, and protection from the elements are the most basic human needs. If you subject guests to a long, drawn-out awards presentation before you feed them, their blood sugar will drop to the point that they will not be able to concentrate on the business at hand. In addition, do not set the tables and chairs so close to one another that you induce claustrophobia. If you have special stage and audience lighting, avoid blinding people with it. And make sure the air conditioning is not freezing the room.

2) When the physiological needs for food, shelter and protection from the elements are reasonably satisfied, address the needs for safety. Structure the awards presentation for success by making it simple enough and rehearsing it enough that the participants do not live in fear of making public fools of themselves. Work with them ahead of the show to give them confidence that the event will run smoothly, and be enjoyable and risk-free to their persons and psyches. Explain to them where they should be at what time, who will prompt them to the stage, how the show will progress, who will escort them to the press room for interviews, etc. If you have disabled guests, prompt them ahead of time on wheelchair access and egress. In short, hold their hands.

3) Having attended to their physiological and safety needs, be considerate of their social needs. Have a reception prior to or after the formal business of the awards so guests can mingle. Have staff or association volunteers on hand to make introductions among guests who do not know each other. As an overall general principle, encourage and facilitate wherever and whenever possible the opportunity for people to "shmooze."

4) Ego needs come next and are of two types: self-esteem and the respect of one's fellows. Rehearse the master of ceremonies to recog-

nize individuals and groups from the stage. Have a photographer take pictures at the tables and of the stage business. Script the proceedings so that introductions of the nominees reflect the respect due them. Make sure the audience is aware of what the awards mean—what the "excellence" is that is being celebrated by the awards themselves.

5) And finally, there are the needs that people have for self-fulfillment. Awards are not an end-all or be-all, but they should confirm in those honored at your awards presentation a sense that they have gone some distance to realizing their own potentialities, and that their achievements point toward opportunities for continued self-development. One of the frustrations of business life is knowing that making employees more productive workers is often related to helping them be more content and appreciative individuals. Awards properly administered and presented can be a powerful resource in achieving that goal.

How to Use Awards to Generate Publicity

Internally, your company can derive innumerable benefits from winning an award or giving one to recognize employees' performance. But the benefits can increase exponentially if you let the outside world know about your achievements—or the achievements your company has chosen to reward.

Giving or getting an award presents myriad marketing opportunities. The tough part can be making the time and resources available to use these opportunities to your company's best advantage. And yet, any effort you make on this front should pay off in a substantial way.

Surely everyone in America has heard of the Good Housekeeping Seal of Approval. Wouldn't you like your awards program to have that kind of name recognition? Promotion and marketing are the keys.

First, think publicity. Get your communications specialist geared up to write press releases and lots of them—or hire an outside public relations firm, if necessary.

Don't let these opportunities for "free ink" pass your company by. After all, editorial coverage in newspapers, newsletters and magazines costs you nothing

Start Sending Out Press Releases

(except the price of a press release, a stamp and possibly a phone interview)—and it is almost always worth far more than any amount of advertising you can buy. Why? It has credibility.

The key is getting the releases out early. For instance, monthly magazines typically have a two- or three-month "lead time"—the time from a magazine's editorial deadlines until it arrives in readers' hands. Publications aren't going to run old news—especially a call for entries—so get your press releases out as early as you can. (If your deadlines are tight, try focusing your efforts on weekly titles and daily papers.)

If you are putting on an "external" awards program, you have several opportunities to send out press releases and generate some publicity. For instance, you can alert the media to:

- a call for entries;

- an announcement of the nominees;

- a call for votes (if voting is open to customers of a large chain, for example);

- the awards ceremony; and, of course,

- the winners.

If you have an "internal" awards program, you can send out press releases that explain which of your employees has received an award and why. You probably will want to interview the award winners, too, and send their photos and quotes along with the press releases.

If you are the recipient of an award, you'll want to alert the media, and again include quotes from key personnel. If possible, also include quotes from people who were involved in judging the award or in developing it—or at least include a contact name and number for the sanctioning organization.

In short, the easier you make it for smaller newspapers and magazines to put together an article on your company, the more likely it is that they will run one. So, your press releases should be brief, but they should include as much pertinent information about the award as possible. This might include:

- a brief description of the group that presented the award (whether it is an association, a charity or your company);

- the values or qualities that the award promotes and rewards;

- the criteria for winning;

- the reason the particular company, employee or product won;

- what winning this award means to your company (or your employee);

- anything else that is pertinent, unusual or newsworthy.

Announcing the Nominees

For any awards program, the announcement of nominees should be in written form—normally a press release. They also may be announced "live." A sample of a Primetime Emmy Awards press release cover sheet announcing the nominations appears in Appendix 4.

This press release includes not only the five nominees in each category, it also has other pertinent information about the show. The example below, for Outstanding Comedy Series, includes the network that broadcast the program, the production company responsible for the show and the names of the Emmy-eligible producers. (This information is purposefully left off the ballots—so voters can concentrate on the quality of the programs themselves, rather than the personalities or companies behind them.)

1995 Primetime Emmy Awards Nominations: Outstanding Comedy Series

Frasier

NBC

Grub Street Productions in association with Paramount Network Television

Peter Casey, David Angell, David Lee, Christopher Lloyd, Executive Producers; Vic Rauseo, Linda Morris, Co-Executive Producers; Maggie Randell, Elias Davis, David Pollock, Producers; Chuck Ranberg, Anne Flett-Giordano, Joe Keenan, Co-Producers

In addition, the press release has a preface to the category-by-category listing of nominations that gives a statistical rundown of the number of nominations for each network and program. Other information given to the press (but not part of the press release itself) includes a list of the categories for which each program is nominated and an A-Z list of the names of the nominees. All of these documents are drawn directly from the database that was built from information on the entry forms.

Another press-friendly accompaniment to the roster of nominations is a collection of trivia about the awards, past and present. (The complete list for a recent Primetime Emmys, including the names of winners and winning shows, appears in Appendix 5.) Here are a few sample categories:

- Most nominations for an individual
- Most nominations for a program
- Most Emmys won by a series
- Most Emmys won by a series in a single season
- Emmy winners who have also won Oscars (performers only)
- Husbands and wives who have both won Emmys
- Parents and children who have both won Emmys

Whatever "facts and figures" trivia you include as a supplement to your press release, customize it to your target media. For instance, if you are announcing nominations for a sports legends charity award, cite statistics about the careers of the players you are honoring. If you are announcing nominees for a literary prize, detail the publications and any other awards won by the authors.

The media will be much more likely to notice your nominations if they include interesting "sidebar" information that could be used to embellish an otherwise bland report.

Live Announcement

If the nomination press release is accompanied by a live announcement, then it should be scripted. In the case of the announcement of the Primetime Emmy nominations, the ceremony is designed for television broadcast. Portions of the 1995 announcement ceremony appear in Appendix 6.

It's a good idea to use slides during the live announcement so the audience can quickly and easily recognize each of the individuals, shows or products being nominated. You can get these slides from a representative of the entrant.

Here is a sample letter soliciting slides from a network representative for the Primetime Emmys:

> Once again, the Academy is planning an impressive audio-visual presentation for this year's Primetime Emmy Awards nomination announcement ceremony on July 18, 1996.
>
> To help us prepare for every possibility of nomination, we need your cooperation. Please send color slides of the attached list of performers. The list contains the names of the Emmy entrants from shows on your network in the lead actor and actress in comedy series, drama series and miniseries/ Movies of the Week categories. All slides will be returned.
>
> We request that the slides be sent to us by July 12.
>
> Please note we are preparing for every eventuality with this request. A request for slides is in no way an indication of probable nominations.
>
> Thank you.

Anyone who has watched the Primetime Emmy Awards presentation or the Academy Awards show knows that the press turns out in force for these events. There are paparazzi taking pictures of the nominees and presenters and other noteworthy guests as they arrive. There are TV and radio personalities interviewing them. There is tremendous buildup before the actual awards presentation. And then, the moment we've all been waiting for: The entire (or at least the better part of the) awards presentation is shown live.

While business awards outside the entertainment industry don't generate this kind of excitement among the general public, your awards certainly should be exciting to some group of people and companies. And you will want to use this interest in the same way the entertainment industry does: to stimulate interest in award-winning products and companies.

There are several ways to do this, many of which involve alerting the media. As we've already noted, in most cases, it is vital to send out press releases at each step along the way. But you should get even more coverage of the awards and the award winners if you invite the press to attend your awards presentation.

You'll want to send out your press invitations when you invite the nominees. In fact, it's a good idea to include a press release listing the nominees along with the invitations for members of the media.

The invitation should lay the ground rules for media members who will be covering the event, too. You'll want to let them know:

- who, what, when, where, how and why;

- if they will have special seating or parking arrangements;

- if they will be allowed to bring cameras to the event;

- if photos of the winners will be provided;

- if there will be a formal session at which they can interview winners, or if they should arrive early to talk to the nominees;

- what to wear (many journalists dress quite informally around the office, and will want to be dressed appropriately for your event—and you are the one who knows best what "appropriately" will mean).

If you will be allowing photographers at the awards ceremonies, you will need to work out the logistics so photographers can get the shots they need and other attendees can still see the proceedings. You may even want to issue press credentials that members of the media can pin or clip on, so any security people you have hired or maitre d's know who should be milling about by the stage and who should remain seated during the presentations.

Who to Invite

Your budget may dictate how many members of the media you can invite to your awards presentation. (You may need to create an A list and a B list—such that members of the B list only get press releases.) Ideally, you will want to invite everyone who does regular coverage of your industry. This would include editors of trade magazines and even newsletters that cover your field.

You also may want to invite reporters and photographers from the local newspapers, a representative of your college's alumni magazine or paper, or even local college newspaper staffers.

Perhaps the more mainstream media will have an interest in your awards presentation, as well. If you can put together a press release or an invitation that clarifies the interest for these newspapers' or magazines' readers, the editors probably will at least consider attending (especially if you're going to be serving food).

There may even be a cable TV show that addresses your industry these days. In that case, you'll want to add the show's hosts to the invite list.

Other Ways You Can Promote the Awards Program

If you have a site on the Internet, you certainly will want to cover the awards program there—publishing a call for entries, the rules (at least an abbreviated version), a list of nominees and the winners.

You also can post photos and descriptions of nominees and winners, which are particularly appealing in the case of design awards. Literary awards programs could post excerpts from nominated and winning books and articles. The sound and video capabilities of the Internet open up other possibilities, as well.

You also could send videotapes to the media, including background information and the awards presentation—which could, conceivably, make it onto a cable TV show in edited form.

Ways Recipients Will Promote the Award

If you have succeeded in creating an award that is desirable and respected, you can expect the recipients to do plenty of promotion of the award on their own.

However, there are ways that you can make this easier for them.

You can provide them with:

- award nominee and award winner logos for them to use;

- post-award certificates and citations;

- videotapes and photos of the awards presentation; and

- program books from the awards presentation.

Providing and Designing Logos

We have mentioned awards logos a couple times during the course of this book. Winners can affix these logos to their packaging—either by designing the logo into a new package or by affixing a sticker to existing packaging. (You may want to provide stickers, as well.)

Affixing awards logos to packaging has benefits for the award recipient, because it positions the winning product as a superior example in its category. As we've said before, in an era of overwhelming choices, awards help consumers and businessess sort through the clutter and find noteworthy products and service providers.

These logos also have benefits for the award giver. They promote your awards program—and position the award as something of value in your industry or the retail community at large. They also encourage other companies to compete for your award in the future, so that they may affix the logo to their packaging and level the playing field for consumers'—or businesses'— dollars.

Recipients also are likely to mention the award in their television and print advertising. You can make this easier by providing a logo for use here, as well.

Think about how many times you have seen an automobile ad that mentions Car of the Year honors. Several magazines give these awards—and each one benefits whenever a recipient mentions the magazine's name in conjunction with the award in its advertising.

When designing your awards logo, you will want to give some indication of the criteria for winning the award—in as few words as possible. That way, people who will buy the product on the basis of its "award-winning" status can be sure they are getting what they expect. After all, all awards are not created equal. An award for photographic quality in a magazine does not guarantee editorial quality. An award for speed does not guarantee durability. And an award for artistic merit does not always guarantee wholesome values, as some parents have discovered—a little too late.

Post-Awards Certificates

You also may want to make post-awards certificates available to the winners. There are three kinds of post-awards certificates:

- appreciation certificates issued by the charity, association or business that sponsored the award to those individuals and companies that contributed to its success;

- craft citations that an award winner may give out in recognition of those individuals who materially contributed to the award-winning achievement; and

- commemorative versions of the awards themselves that an award winner may give out to a limited and select number of individuals or companies, without whose contributions the award never would have been won. These commemoratives are meant for—and usually wind up in—corporate trophy cases.

The very idea of printing the name of your company or association on a plaque, certificate or statuary logo and installing it in a prominent place in the office of an important industry colleague is out of the question in all contexts, except awards. What individual or company does not have a "wall of fame" displaying honors?

Furthermore, the opportunity for the recipient to pass on to others certificates of appreciation for contributions made toward the winning of the award spreads his or her fame along with your name. Although there may be some costs for these followup items, they usually are well worth the benefits of having your award displayed so prominently and with such pride.

Craft Citations

If you are going to offer craft citations to award recipients, they will need to mention the award and the winner.

For example, the following information appears on Emmy Award craft citations:

Academy of Television Arts & Sciences

1995-1996 Primetime Emmy Awards

Honors

Mary Manhardt

For Contributions to the Emmy Award-Winning
Achievement

Outstanding Informational Series

TV Nation

NBC

[President's signature]

You also will need to send an order form for craft
citations to each award winner. Here is a sample form:

Emmy Award Craft Citations

As an Emmy Award winner, you may wish to recognize individuals (generally assistants) who materially contributed to your Emmy-winning
achievement. For those select people, the Television Academy offers handsome "Craft Citations"
upon your request.

Craft Citations are 8¹/₂x11 inches, with an
Emmy at the center. Each citation is personalized
as follows:

1995-1996 Primetime Emmy Awards

Honors [name of contributor]

for contributions to the Emmy Award

in [category, program title, network]

The first five citations are free. Each additional is
$xx.

Craft Citations may only be ordered by Emmy Award winners. To request citations, please complete and return this form to the Academy office. Citations will be sent to you for distribution. Please allow approximately 6 to 8 weeks for delivery.

Your Name _____

Program Title _____

Category _____

Address _____

Phone _____

Please send me craft citation(s) for the following:

(Please check spelling and type or print clearly)

1. _____

2. _____

3. _____

4. _____

5. _____

Attach a separate typed sheet for additional names.

Commemorative Awards

Award winners generally can order as many craft citations as they would like. While these citations should look impressive, they should not look like the actual award.

Commemorative awards, on the other hand, look a lot more like the actual award—or may even be a duplicate of the real thing. Therefore, they should be given out far more sparingly.

For instance, Emmy-winning producers may order *one* commemorative Emmy Award on behalf of the studio, production company or network that was principally involved with the winning program. Commemorative Emmys cannot be ordered for individuals. (A total of three commemorative Emmys may be ordered.)

The intent of issuing commemorative Emmys is to give studios, production companies and networks the opportunity to display, in a corporate or public space, the Emmy Awards for programs that they engaged and/or broadcast.

All commemorative Emmy orders are subject to the approval of the Primetime Awards Committee.

A commemorative Emmy is engraved as follows:

1995 Primetime Emmy Awards
[category]

[program title]

[if a miniseries or special, broadcast date(s)]

[name of studio, production company or network]

Commemorative Emmys will have "commemorative" engraved on the engraving band (180 degrees around from the above engraving).

Again, there is a charge for commemorative Emmys. If you decide to make commemorative awards available to your company's winners, you will want to charge at least enough for them to cover your production and shipping costs.

The advantage of favorable publicity over advertising is that people tend to believe what they read in

The Power of
Publicity

editorial copy or television reports more than they believe what is claimed in ads.

Similarly, the advantage of spreading the news of your award via certificates, citations, commemoratives and other followup items comes from their expression of the recipient's "pride of ownership," which is something any kind of money—even advertising dollars—cannot buy. For example, automobile makers can only describe the satisfaction that might be gained from owning one of their vehicles in their ads—but the J.D. Power automotive awards are based on consumer testimony of that satisfaction.

Publicity works when there is a "hook" to catch the attention of the intended audience. Awards publicity hooks its audience with the promise of something extraordinary, because awards, by definition, separate the extraordinary from the clutter of the ordinary. This is the principle that drives all publicity about awards programs and their recipients, and it is the reason why the most important and prestigious awards receive the most publicity. So, if you want more favorable publicity, plan and implement better awards programs.

Conclusion

Implementing the basic principles of awards in a successful awards program requires a practical method. The Deming method of total quality management, which serves as the core criteria for the prestigious Deming Prize, outlines 14 points of "management by positive cooperation" (discussed in Chapter 6).

These same points can be adapted to awards administration:

1) Create constancy of purpose for improvement of product and service—*i.e., identify the mission of the award and customize it to fulfill that mission.*

2) Adopt the new philosophy: Mistakes and negativism are unacceptable—*i.e., structure the awards theory (rules) and practice (procedures) for success.*

3) Cease dependence on mass inspection. Require instead statistical evidence that quality is built in to eliminate the need for inspection on a mass basis—*i.e., set up a redundancy-laden, step-by-step proofing system that targets specific errors and preserves the corrected copy from subsequent contamination.*

4) End the practice of awarding business on the basis of price tag alone. Instead, depend on meaningful measures of quality along with price—*i.e., pay the price for reliable vendors (printers, accountants, hotels, etc.) and infra-structure (computers, software, etc.).*

5) Improve constantly and forever the system of production and service—*i.e., design a checks and balances awards process review system that is ongoing, proactive and reactive.*

6) Institute a vigorous training program of edu-cation and retraining—*i.e., regularly review awards rules, procedures and case-by-case pre-cedents.*

7) Institute leadership—*i.e., know the awards process well enough to confidently guide vol-unteers and staff through its myriad twists and turns to its successful completion.*

8) Drive out fear so that everyone may work effectively for the company—*i.e., recognize that the implementation of a successful awards process is so complicated and tricky that there is no room for anything but full cooperation among all parties.*

9) Break down barriers between departments—*i.e., facilitate and be politically sensitive to the interaction of awards with membership, activi-ties, finance, committees and others involved in the sponsoring organization.*

10) Eliminate numerical goals, posters and slogans for the work force that ask for new levels of productivity without providing new methods—*i.e., to increase the specific value of awards, decrease general misconceptions about awards.*

11) Eliminate work standards that prescribe numerical quotas—*i.e., when budgeting the time and resources necessary for the completion of any phase of the competition, weigh both the complexity and the bulk of the task.*

12) Remove barriers to pride of workmanship—*i.e., design rules and procedures in a way that volunteers and staff can successfully implement them.*

13) Encourage education and self-improvement for everyone—*i.e., budget enough time to allow everyone involved in both the planning and implementation of awards programs to keep up with the often unpredictable arc of the learning curve.*

14) Take action to accomplish the transformation—*i.e., cultivate the volunteers, hire the staff, buy the computers and software, contract the vendors, work with the consultants, cooperate with the other departments, make "wiggle room" for contingencies—and pray.*

Whether the award is the Bald Is Beautiful prize given by the Bald Headed Men of America Association, the Hooker of the Year Award from the National Tractor Pullers Association or the Emmy Award from the Academy of Television Arts & Sciences, the basic principles of awards are the same. Those principles—and their total quality management—are the foundation for building respect for any association, business or charity's existing or planned awards program.

Implemented properly, the principles and techniques discussed in this book are the means to bridging the gap between the theory of the valuable role that awards can play and the practice of successful awards programs.

As an official for a leading company in the business of structuring corporate recognition programs puts it, "When you see someone hug and kiss the award, that's what it's all about."

Appendix 1

Here is an example of the Achievement of Excellence judging format that includes categories of evaluation:

Official 1995 Emmy Judging Panel Ballot
Outstanding Achievement in Special Visual Effects

Vote "Yes—it should receive an Emmy" or "No—it should not receive an Emmy" for each of the entrants.

Any entry that receives 2/3 of the total votes cast for it as "Yes" votes win an Emmy.

Use the following categories of evaluation to guide your decisions.

1. Do the Special Visual Effects look real, or convincing in the intended context? Do they look like part of the same production as the live action portions? Has linear and aerial perspective been taken into consideration? Is the lighting direction and intensity consistent within each shot? Do the colors in the shots look right together?

2. Are the optical or electronic composites of the highest quality? Are there any apparent matte lines around elements? Do the various elements in the shots seem properly blended together? Are the contrast ratios and color intensities consistent?

3. Do the visual effects fit within the dramatic context of the story? Do they serve to move the story along, or are they there for their own sake? How well do they help tell the story?

4. In the case of motion control miniatures: Are the moves natural for the object being depicted? Is the lighting consistent with the environment of the background? Do the structural details and painting on the models make them convincing as full-sized objects?

5. Effects animation: Does it really look like part of the scene? Does it match any reactive lighting in the background? Is the motion natural? Are the colors and transparency or opacity appropriate?

6. Matte paintings: How perfectly does the painted portion blend in with any live action portions? Does it look like reality? How does it fit in with the live action shots that surround it?

7. Blue screen composites: How accurately does the lighting and perspective match between the blue screen and background elements? Is the shadow density consistent? Is there any "fringing" around people or objects in the composite?

8. Have there been any innovative uses of technology that push the envelope of visual effects achievement?

9. Have the shots been designed and executed with an exceptionally high level of artistry?

Appendix 2

1995-1996 Primetime Emmy Awards
Official Entry Form

1. Name, phone and fax number of the eligible person making this entry. (Entries can be made by the producer of an eligible program or by an individual entering himself/herself, or on behalf of his/her team.)

Name _____

Phone _____

Fax _____

Signature _____

2. Check here if you are a producer entering for his/her program, or on behalf of an individual who worked on your program (performer, director, hairstylist, etc.)

3. Entry number. [Your office phone's 7-digit number. If you wish to submit a second entry, photocopy this form and make a new entry number by adding "-2" after the 7th digit of your phone number, "-3" for a third entry, etc.]

4. Category number. [See rules book for categories of competition and their assigned numbers. The Acad-

emy Awards Committee has final determination of category placement of all entries.]

5. Title of series, special (one night) or miniseries (two or more nights).

6. Title of series episode or part of miniseries chosen for submission. [Supporting performers for regular series, list two episodes.]

7. Date(s) and time(s) of first eligible Primetime showing. [Eligible period: June 1, 1995, to May 31, 1996; 6 p.m. to 2 a.m. Supporting performers for regular series, list the airdates of the two episodes you are submitting.]

8. National network on which it was shown.

9. Running time. [Approximate, without commercials.]

10. Program synopsis. [25 words or less. Lead and supporting performers for regular series and series entries for programs need not supply a synopsis. Please note: Any synopsis over 25 words will be edited by the Academy. Producers of MOWs and miniseries entries: Please list the names of the principal leads at the end of your synopsis.]

11. Production company (for example, an "X" production in association with "Y" studio).

12. Entrants: name, on-air credit, address and phone

number of all entrant(s). If you are the person making this entry and are also one of the eligible entrants, please include yourself in the complete list of entrants. [For larger team entries, please attach a separate typed sheet of paper.]

Name _____

On-Air Credit _____

Address _____

Phone _____

13. Performer entrants, please list your character name.

14. Performer entrants in regular series categories: How many episodes did you appear in during the eligibility year? [6/1/95—5/31/96]

15. Makeup and Hairstyling Categories 27 & 28 and 31 & 32: Entries must be accompanied by a 50-word or less statement of the techniques employed in the execution of your achievement. [Please attach a separate typed sheet.]

16. Music entrants: If this entry is for Category 36, please list the song title.

17. Sound entrants: List name of sound house and phone number.

18. Entry fees: $300 (program); $100 (single individual); $200 (2-4 individuals); $300 (5-8 individuals); $400 (9 or more individuals).

Please note: Member vouchers are non-transferable. Full payment (by means of money, vouchers or a combination of money and vouchers) must accompany this entry form. The value of the voucher is calculated by dividing the amount of the entry fee by the number of entrants, i.e., \$200/4 entrants = \$50 value of voucher. Please see pages 13-15 of the Rules Book or the back of your voucher for further instructions on how to calculate this value.

Late entry fees: Nominations will be announced on July 18, and the deadline for errors or omissions is July 22. Except for cases where the omission of a name is an Academy error, no names will be added after July 22. There will be a flat fee of \$150 for each individual added between July 18 and July 22.

A faxed copy of the front page of this entry, stamped with the date that ATAS received it, will be your receipt that the entry was received by the Academy. If you do not receive the faxed receipt within 10 days of submitting the entry form, call the Academy.

19. Voting: You must be a member of ATAS by April 26, 1996, in order to vote in this year's competition. Please contact the Membership Department for an application. See pages 59-62 of the Rules and Procedures booklet for a guide to which peer groups receive which ballots.

Please note: All informational programming categories are voted on by the Informational Programming branch only. If you are a member of another peer group, you must contact the Membership Department by May 3 in order to qualify to receive the Informational Programming Ballot.

Appendix 3

Call for Entries
The 1995-1996 Primetime Emmy Award
for Outstanding Achievement in
Engineering Development

The Awards

The *Emmy Award* to an individual, a company or an organization for developments in engineering that are either so extensive an improvement on existing methods or so innovative in nature that they materially affect the transmission, recording or reception of television. Emmy(s) to winner(s). Possibility of one, more than one or no award.

The *Emmy Plaque* for those achievements that exhibit a high level of engineering and are important to the progress of the industry. The Plaque is not meant to be a consolation prize, but a positive recognition of engineering achievements that are on a different level of technology and industry importance than the Emmy Award. Plaque(s) to winner(s). Possibility of one, more than one or no award.

Entry Procedure

Complete and return the attached form by May 1,

1996. After reviewing the attached form, the committee will request more information, if necessary. Do not send brochures, demo tapes, etc., unless requested.

Contest Procedure

A Blue Ribbon Panel of highly qualified engineers in television will consider engineering developments and determine which, if any, merit an Emmy or a plaque. Awards, if any, will be announced in July 1996.

Academy of Television Arts & Sciences
48th Annual Primetime Emmy Awards
Outstanding Achievement in
Engineering Development

Official Entry Form for Award Consideration

Please complete and return to the Academy by May 1, 1996.

Entry to Be Considered

Name and title of person to be contacted regarding this entry:

Name of company _____
Street address _____
City, state and ZIP code _____
Phone _____

Date of invention _____

Has application been filed for patent? __ Yes __ No

Serial number of application _____

Date of filing _____

If patent has been issued, enclose one (1) copy with this form.

Patent Number _____

Date Issued _____

Name(s) of primary inventor(s) or developer(s) to be credited for this achievement (if not stated on patent).

_____

_____

_____

Above individuals still living? __ Yes __ No

Eligible entries must have been utilized on a nationally televised program. Give the program(s) and broadcast date(s).

_____

_____

_____

Does the item duplicate a similar or earlier device?
__ Yes __ No
(If yes, please include details.) _____

_____

_____

Is invention/technology currently involved in a litigation proceeding? __ Yes __ No
(If yes, please include details.) _____

_____

_____

_____

In a brief paragraph, please explain how this entry advances the state of the art.

_____

_____

_____

_____

_____

_____

Appendix 4

Here is a sample of a Primetime Emmy Awards press release cover sheet announcing the nominations. Explanatory notes are in boldface italics.

July 20, 1995   Contact: John Leverence
5:39 a.m./PDT   Awards Director
(news embargo time)

Note date of release and, if it is time sensitive, the hour and minute it can be released from a news embargo. In the case of this release, a number of the nominations were being announced on **CBS Good Morning** *during a segment that was scheduled to begin at 8:39 a.m./EDT—three hours ahead of West Coast time.*

Always have a contact and phone number, so there is a central source of information for followup inquiries about the information in the press release.

1994-1995 Primetime Emmy Awards
Nominations

The lead paragraph describes what happened at the live nomination announcement.

Nominations for the 47th Annual Primetime Emmy Awards for the period of June 1, 1994, through May 31, 1995, were announced today (July 20) by the Academy of Television Arts & Sciences (ATAS) from the Academy Plaza Theater, North Hollywood, California. ATAS President Richard H. Frank presided, assisted by Betty White, winner of five previous Emmy Awards.

The network summary of Emmy nominations is an at-a-glance review of what follows in the body of the press release—e.g., the category-by-category listing of the nominations.

A total of 354 nominations, compiled by the independent accounting firm of Ernst & Young, were distributed as follows:

A&E—2
ABC—39
CBS—85
Cinemax—1
The Cartoon Network—1
Comedy Central—3
The Discovery Channel—1
The Disney Channel—10
The Family Channel—1
Fox—17
HBO—48
MTV—5
NBC—85
Nickelodeon—1
PBS—17

Showtime—1
Syndicated—7
TNT—17
TBS—5
UPN—7
USA—1

Special circumstances about the competition are noted in the following paragraphs.

Nominations for Outstanding Special Visual Effects will be announced August 14.

There are several juried awards that will be announced in August. With a possibility of one, more than one or no award in each, they are Outstanding Voice-Over Performance, Outstanding Individual Achievement in Animation and Outstanding Achievement in Engineering Development.

Additional Board of Governors Awards yet to be announced are The Syd Cassyd Founders Award and The Governors Award.

Rules and procedures are sketched out below.

Nominations were made by active Academy members who voted for programs and other peer categories of their expertise. For example, performers, in addition to voting for programs, voted for performers, while writers voted for writers, directors for directors, etc.

Peer panels, made up primarily of active Academy members and some other individuals distinguished in their particular fields, will screen nominations during the month of August in the Los Angeles area and, in secret ballot, select the Emmy winners.

The ultimate result of those rules and procedures— the presentation of the Emmys—follows.

The awards presentation telecast—awarding Emmys in 27 categories before a black-tie audience— will be televised by the Fox Television Network on Sunday, September 10, from the Pasadena (California) Civic Auditorium. A host will be named in the coming weeks. Executive producer of the Emmy telecast is Don Mischer. Director is Louis J. Horvitz. The Academy's Governors Ball follows the telecast at the Pasadena Exhibition Hall, adjacent to the auditorium.

On Saturday, September 9, at the Pasadena Exhibition Hall, 53 out of this year's 80 Primetime Emmy categories' awards (primarily in creative arts categories) will be handed out at a black-tie banquet.

Journalists find statistical summaries useful for comparative analyses of nominations.

A complete list of nominations is attached. Editors: See inside summary pages for programs with multiple nominations.

Additional outlets for the press release:

This TV Academy press release, and other recent and future releases, are available via the Academy's electronic mail information-on-demand service. Send E-mail to releases@emmys.org with the word INFO in the body of your message to receive instructions on how to automatically receive press releases, and how to retrieve recent releases from Academy archives.

The full list of nominations in the 47th Annual Primetime Emmy Awards competition is also available on ATAS's World Wide Web site on the Internet, located at http://www.emmys.org/. In addition to the Primetime Emmy nominations, the site will include awards information (facts about past winners, rules, deadlines, trivia, etc.) and details on the Academy's many activities and programs, including news and information about the Television Hall of Fame, College Television Awards, Summer Internship Program, *Emmy Magazine* and Academy Activities.

The press release listing nominations in the Top 10 Categories appears in Appendix 6.

A press-friendly accompaniment to the roster of nominations for the Emmy Awards is a collection of trivia about the awards (past and present). The 1995 list follows.

1995 Primetime Emmy Awards—
Emmy Facts & Figures
(Emmy Statistics Through the 1995 Nominations)

~~~~~~

SUMMARY OF "MOST" EMMYS

~~~~~~

MOST NOMINATIONS FOR AN INDIVIDUAL:
Dwight Hemion—(42)
George Stevens, Jr.—(31)
Jan Scott—(29)
Alan Alda—(28)
Don Mischer—(28)
Steven Bochco—(28)
Buz Kohan—(27)
George Schaefer—(25)

MOST NOMINATIONS FOR A PROGRAM:
Cheers—(117)
M*A*S*H—(109)
Hill Street Blues—(98)

MOST EMMYS WON BY INDIVIDUALS:
Dwight Hemion—(16)
Buz Kohan—(13)
Jan Scott—(11)
Ian Fraser—(11)
Don Mischer—(11)
Steven Bochco—(9)
Carl Reiner—(8)
Mary Tyler Moore—(8)

MOST EMMYS WON BY A SERIES:
The Mary Tyler Moore Show—(29)
Cheers—(27)
Hill Street Blues—(26)
The Carol Burnett Show—(25)

MOST EMMYS WON BY A MINISERIES:
Roots—(9)

MOST EMMYS WON BY A MOVIE OF THE WEEK:
Eleanor and Franklin—(11)

MOST EMMYS WON BY A SERIES IN A SINGLE SEASON:
Hill Street Blues (Premiere Season)—(8)

EMMY WINNERS WHO HAVE ALSO WON OSCARS (PERFORMERS ONLY)

Jack Albertson
Ingrid Bergman
Shirley Booth
Marlon Brando
Art Carney
Bette Davis
Melvyn Douglas
Patty Duke
Sally Field
Jane Fonda
Ruth Gordon
Louis Gossett, Jr.
Lee Grant
Helen Hayes
Katharine Hepburn
Dustin Hoffman
William Holden
Holly Hunter
Glenda Jackson
Cloris Leachman
Karl Malden
Thomas Mitchell
Rita Moreno
Laurence Olivier
Geraldine Page
Vanessa Redgrave
Jason Robards
Cliff Robertson

Eva Marie Saint
George C. Scott
Paul Scofield
Simone Signoret
Maureen Stapleton
Meryl Streep
Barbra Streisand
Jessica Tandy
Claire Trevor
Peter Ustinov
Shelley Winters
Joanne Woodward
Loretta Young

HUSBANDS AND WIVES WHO HAVE BOTH WON EMMYS

Marlo Thomas and Phil Donahue
Bonnie Bartlett and William Daniels
Colleen Dewhurst and George C. Scott
Lynn Fontanne and Alfred Lunt
Jessica Tandy and Hume Cronyn
Lynn Whitfield and Brian Gibson

PARENTS AND CHILDREN WHO HAVE BOTH WON EMMYS

Danny and Marlo Thomas
James and Tyne Daly
Carl and Rob Reiner

EMMY WINNER WHO IS "MOST HONORED INDIVIDUAL IN THE ENTERTAINMENT INDUSTRY"

From the *Los Angeles Times*, December 3, 1996:

Bob Hope has received a framed citation from the *Guiness Book of World Records* for having had "the longest continuous contract in the history of radio and television"—60 years with NBC. The 93-year-old native of London received the citation at his Palm Springs home; London-based *Guiness Book* officials flew out to present it to him. This was Hope's second Guiness record: He was enshrined earlier this decade as "The Most Honored Individual in the Entertainment Industry" after receiving more than 100 national and international honors, 53 of which were academic honors. He has received four special Academy Awards, an Emmy [in 1996 for Outstanding Variety Special, *Chrysler Presents the Bob Hope Christmas Special*], a Peabody, an Order of the British Empire and Distinguished Service medals from all branches of the armed forces.

Here is a sample of a Primetime Emmy Awards press release announcing the nominations. Explanatory notes are in boldface italics.

Academy of Television Arts & Sciences
47th Annual Primetime Emmy Awards

Announcement of Nominations in the
Top 10 Categories

5:38 a.m.
July 20, 1995
Academy Theatre

The above header identifies the event, time and place. This is followed by a "short rundown" of the nominations being read aloud in the live announcement:

1. Drama Series
2. Comedy Series
3. Made for Television Movie

4. Miniseries
5. Lead Actress, Miniseries or a Special
6. Lead Actor, Miniseries or a Special
7. Lead Actress, Drama Series
8. Lead Actor, Drama Series
9. Lead Actress, Comedy Series
10. Lead Actor, Comedy Series

SCRIPT

Because the announcement of the Emmy nominations is televised, it is useful to the press in the auditorium to understand the ground rules and procedures. The Academy spokesperson intros the live announcement as follows:

Academy Spokesperson (off air, just before ceremonies begin):

"Your attention please ...

"We'll be starting our nomination ceremony in a few moments—at exactly 5:38 a.m. We'll only announce the Top 10 categories during our ceremony, handing out full nomination announcement packets after that. These packets are printed on white paper. The colored release that is also being handed out will give you updated Emmy background information. Be aware that you should seek out each release.

At the conclusion of the ceremony, the president of the Academy, Richard Frank, and Betty White will be available for additional interviewing, as will the Emmy Show's executive producer, Don Mischer, who is with us in the audience.

Mr. Frank, the Academy president, now steps up to a double podium with Ms. White.

Richard Frank (on air, when cued):
"Good morning. I'm Richard Frank, president of the Academy of Television Arts & Sciences. We're here to announce top nominations for the 47th Annual Primetime Emmys to be telecast by ABC on September 10. We're pleased that five-time Emmy winner Betty White is joining us to announce these nominations."

Betty:
"The nominations in the drama series category are ..."

As the nominations are read, television monitors in the set wall behind Ms. White flash the logos for the nominations. The director switches the line feed (i.e., what is being broadcast) from the podium camera to the monitor feed. As each program is named, its logo appears full-frame on the line feed. After all are announced, the line feed splits five ways to show the logo for each nominated program, then returns to the podium camera for the next category intro.

Chicago Hope
ER
Law & Order
NYPD Blue
The X-Files

Mr. Frank takes the next category, Ms. White the

one after that, and they continue to alternate through the announcement of the program categories. The announcement of the performer categories follows the same pattern, but instead of a program logo, the monitor feed shows a picture of the nominated performer. The entire announcement lasts just a few minutes and concludes with a brief closure announcement:

Rich (at conclusion of announcements):

"That concludes our nomination ceremonies. The Academy press packets listing all other nominees are now available for handout in the rear of the auditorium. Thank you for attending."

Index

Ad & PR Awards Competition Alert 80, 188
Allstate 75-76
American Banker 24
American Music Awards 173
American National Standards Institute (ANSI) 49, 95, 179, 200, 223
application 82-84, 91, 93-94, 103, 136, 140, 175, 196, 198, 237-238, 302-306
association awards 34, 47-63, 96, 133, 198, 240-242
    members only 59, 133
    mission statement 48
    purpose 48, 53, 57, 97-98, 117, 122, 127, 158, 240, 271
Autry, Gene 69
Avon 75-76
Awards, Honors and Prizes 81
awards presentations 253-276
    acceptance speech 6, 66, 262-263
    audio-visual 248, 255-256, 266, 282
    business awards presentations 255
    do's and don'ts 274
    elements 255-256, 261, 271
    inviting the press 282
    photographers 284
    pre-production 256-259, 263
    production 263-271
    recording 271
    talent/entertainment 255, 256, 258
Bald Is Beautiful Award 9, 142, 295
Malcolm Baldrige National Quality Award 8, 81-84, 90-91, 93-95, 104-105, 117, 138-141, 164, 175, 178, 192, 195-196, 236-237, 241, 249-251
    entry form 192-196, 236
ballots 138, 177, 182, 187, 203, 217-219, 223, 227, 229, 231-232, 234, 236, 243-244, 247-248, 280, 302
    distribution 202, 218-219, 233, 247
    preparation 232-233
    verification of legitimacy 219
Banner Pharmacaps 20
beauty contests 162
Blockbuster Entertainment Awards 172
Booker literary prize 10
Bowers Worldwide Travel Management 21
Brooks, Garth 119

budget 114-115, 117, 188, 190, 229, 239-251, 254, 284, 295
    association awards 240-242, 246-249
    charity awards 240
    expenditures 239, 246-250
    income 239-242, 246, 250
    post-awards 239-242
    pre-awards 239, 240, 246
bylaws 55, 115-116
Buchwald, Art 71
BYTE 34-35
CableAce 176
Caldicott Award 124
calendar 10, 11, 117-118, 144-145, 188, 190, 223, 227, 229-230, 233, 236-237
    wiggle room 233, 235, 295
Car Craft All-Star Drag Racing Team awards 230, 254
Car of the Year 7, 287
cash awards 21, 26-27, 63, 171
    grants 198
    prize money 62
    profit-sharing 23
    variable compensation 23
Catalyst Award 75-76
certificates 27, 78, 241-242, 247, 249, 286-288, 292
    appreciation 288
    craft citations 287-290
    post-award 286-290
chamber of commerce 96-97
charity awards 65-73, 113, 122, 240
    that recognize business 70-71
Colson, Chuck 123
commemorative awards 290-291
competitive awards 161, 164-168, 178, 181, 187, 198, 242
    like vs. like 162-164
copyrights 125-127
Corporation for Public Broadcasting 181
Dana Corp. 104
Deming Prize 86, 88-89, 93, 109, 141, 166, 169, 293
    14 points of "management by positive cooperation" 87, 293
de Tocqueville, Alexis 47, 70
Direct Marketing Association 50
Directors Guild of America 12
double-pass system 176-177
Dove Seal 41
Edgars 145
Eli Lilly 103
Emmy Awards 2, 5, 11, 50, 113, 116, 136, 163, 166, 177-178, 184, 189, 203-205, 217, 223-225, 233, 242, 253, 261, 279-280, 282, 288-289, 291, 295, 299, 303-304, 307-308, 311, 313, 319

birth of 50
divorce 55
Engineering Emmy 184, 303-306
Los Angeles area 232-234, 309
name (history of) 5-6
Syd Cassyd Founders Award 116, 172, 309
entry fee 100, 190, 199, 214-215, 217, 241-246, 302
entry form 117, 153, 187-189, 191-192, 195, 198-204, 206, 212-213, 231-232, 236, 247, 280, 302
distribution 13, 107, 117, 125, 200-202, 204, 218, 232, 247-249, 272, 290
gathering information 191
processing 204, 206, 223
receipt confirmation 202
Environmental Media Association 48
ESPY 68
Film Critics Association 147
FirstMerit 30-31
Fluor Daniel 28-29
foundation awards 105
fund-raisers 66
donor dance 70
golf tournaments 65, 67-68
silent auction 66, 240, 261, 265
GO WEST! 41-42
Golden Globe 8, 12-13, 55-56, 121, 153
Golden Mouse Award 34
Good Egg Award 19-20, 70, 113-115, 166, 246, 256-258, 272
Good Housekeeping Seal of Approval 41, 277
Grammy 8, 53, 176, 203-204
HBO 99-100, 205, 308
Heisman Memorial Trophy 173
hierarchy of needs 16
Hill Street Blues 5-6, 11, 313-314
Hollywood Foreign Press Association 55, 121, 153
Hooker of the Year 9, 295
Huston, John 146
IBP Inc. 128-131
In Search of Excellence 18
Industry Week 103-105
International Press Academy 55
Internet 35, 41, 43-45, 56, 60, 80, 123, 173, 285, 311
Proud Eagle Awards 43
Site of the Week 43
ISO 78-79, 92-95
J. Frank Schmidt & Son Co. 27
J.D. Power 39-40, 292
judges 17, 80, 91, 104, 118, 152, 161-186, 222, 223-225, 237, 246, 249
broad-based electorate 171-172, 174, 182, 218
expertise 169-171, 186, 249, 309

    judging panel 163, 180, 213, 226, 232-233, 236, 297
    jury 23, 88, 129, 160, 172, 177, 182, 185, 226
    narrow-based electorate 171, 174, 182, 218
judging formats 177-178, 180, 297
    competitive 161, 164-168, 178, 181, 187, 198, 242
    non-competitive 161, 166-168, 178, 180-183, 185
    preferential voting 180, 222
    quantitative 178, 180
    ratings system 178, 182
Junior Achievement 68-69
Kazan, Elia 147
Kentucky Fried Chicken 57-58
Kenesaw M. Landis Award 170
Loebner Prize 171
logos 125, 286, 321
Lydia Awards 60
magazine awards 34-36, 101-105
Man of the Year 8, 39, 71-72
Marconi Radio Awards 59
marketing 1, 12, 36, 39, 57, 102, 126, 188, 204, 229, 277
Maslow, A.H. 16, 274
Mason, Jackie 148-152
McCaw Cellular Communications 253
Merix Corp. 84
Microsoft 33-34
Miller, Dennis 205-206, 212
minority-owned businesses 98
myths 121
National Book Award 8, 10-11
National Institute of Packaging, Handling and Logistics Engineers (NIPHLE) 49
National Tree Farmer of the Year 58
Newbery Medal 124
New England Telephone (NET) 154-159
Newsweek Editor's Choice Awards 41-42
Nobel Prize 8, 106-108
nominees 17, 42, 60, 68, 121, 150, 163, 172-177, 206, 217, 220-221, 223-226, 231-232, 234, 241, 243, 245-246, 249, 262, 271-272, 276, 278-281, 283-285, 322
non-competitive awards 161, 166-168, 178, 180-183, 185
open-ended awards program 19
Oscar 8, 12-13, 52-53, 121, 125-127, 137-138, 144, 170, 173-174, 219
    name (history of) 5-6
Peabody 8, 99-100, 317
Pioneer Industries 77-78
Pontiac Master Sales Guild 22
post mortem 226-227
press release 37, 102, 201, 206, 223-224, 226, 234, 246-247, 249, 277-285, 307-311, 319-322
    awards ceremony 37, 226, 278
    call for entries 48-49, 187, 200-201, 229, 278, 285, 303

    call for votes 278
    embargo time 307
    nominees 223-224, 278-283, 307-311, 319-322
    photos 278
    quotes 278
    statistics 281
    trivia 281, 313-317
    winners 278-279
proofing entries 207-208, 211-212, 217, 229, 293
    inconsistent categorization proof 210
    multiple entry proof 208-209
    network proof 212
    program title proof 207
    proofing for "special rules" errors 190, 206, 212
publicity 34, 36, 40, 53, 121, 243, 246-249, 277-292
purpose, awards' 5, 13-14, 43, 48, 53, 57, 97-98, 117, 122, 127, 158, 240, 253, 271, 293
Pulitzer 8, 140, 172, 191-192
recognition 5, 7, 11-18, 20-21, 23, 25-28, 30, 38, 43, 50, 53, 56, 58-59, 96, 98, 100, 104, 113-
    114, 116, 122, 151, 166, 187-188, 239, 243, 250, 257, 277, 287, 296, 303
    need for recognition 16
respect 11, 29, 56, 120-121, 253, 259-261, 276, 285, 295
restrictions 136-145, 188
    age 136, 137, 145
    moral suitability 136-137, 145-147
    multiple application 136, 140
    principal identity 136-137, 141-142
    prior achievement 136, 137, 143
    quantity restriction 136-140
    special case 136
    time frame 136, 137, 144
Rinder Printing 97
Rose Parade 181-182
safety awards 27-28, 101, 128, 130
San Francisco International Film Festival 183
scholarships 50, 242
Screen Actors Guild Awards 174
script 225, 263-271
Shanghai Television Festival 146, 172
Shine 12-13
Shingo Prize 85
Silicon Graphics 18
Harry Singh & Sons 131
single-pass system 177
Soap Opera Digest Award 175
Society of Plastics Engineers 53, 242
Spielberg, Steven 13, 72
"spirit" awards 19, 69-70, 72, 139
Sports Legends 66-68, 263, 267-268, 270, 281

And the Winner Is ...

Star Award 125-127
state-based awards 90
Steinman, Jim 203-204
Terryberry Co. 20, 259
ties 183, 187, 219-223
Timken 26
Tony 8, 148-152
total quality management (TQM) 26, 86, 166, 250, 293, 295
university awards 98-100
value of awards 121, 295
vendor awards 61
Victor Sports Awards 67
voting 37, 62, 161, 173-176, 180, 182, 187, 217, 219-220, 222-223, 226, 231-233, 236, 278, 309
    single-tier 226
    two-tier 174, 217, 226
    three-tier 176
Widget Co. 19-20, 70-71, 115, 138-139, 199, 240, 256-259, 261
    Widgie Award 199-200
women, awards for 76, 98
Working Mother 102-103

Also Available from Merritt Publishing

BUSINESS PLANS TO GAME PLANS
A Practical System for Turning Strategies Into Action

HOW TO FINANCE A GROWING BUSINESS
An Insider's Guide to Negotiating the Capital Markets

HOW TO INSURE YOUR CAR
A Step by Step Guide to Buying the Coverage You Need at Prices You Can Afford

HOW TO INSURE YOUR HOME
A Step by Step Guide to Buying the Coverage You Need at Prices You Can Afford

HOW TO INSURE YOUR LIFE
A Step by Step Guide to Buying the Coverage You Need at Prices You Can Afford

INSURING THE BOTTOM LINE
How to Protect Your Company from Liabilities, Catastrophes, and Other Business Risks

MAKE UP YOUR MIND
Entrepreneurs Talk About Decision Making

MANAGING GENERATION X
How to Bring Out the Best in Young Talent

UNDER 40 FINANCIAL PLANNING
From Graduation to Your First House

MASTERING DIVERSITY
Managing Your Work Force Under ADA and Other Anti-Discrimination Laws

OSHA IN THE REAL WORLD
How to Maintain Workplace Safety while Keeping Your Competitive Edge

RIGHTFUL TERMINATION
Defensive Strategies for Hiring and Firing in the Lawsuit-Happy 90's

TAMING THE LAWYERS
What to Expect in a Lawsuit and How to Make Sure Your Attorney Gets Results

THE OVER 50 INSURANCE SURVIVAL GUIDE
How to Know What You Need, Get What You Want and Avoid Rip-offs

TRUE ODDS
How Risk Affects Your Everyday Life

"WHAT DO YOU MEAN IT'S NOT COVERED?"
A Practical Guide to Understanding Insurance

WORKERS' COMP FOR EMPLOYERS
How to Cut Claims, Reduce Premiums, and Stay Out of Trouble

AND MORE!